ADRIAN LAN

TRUE

CRIME

UK

**REAL CRIMINAL CASES
FROM GREAT BRITAIN**

© 2021 Stefan Waidelich, Zesigweg 6, 72213 Altensteig

The work, including its parts, is protected by copyright. Any use outside the narrow limits of the copyright law is not permitted without the consent of the copyright holder and the author. This applies in particular to the electronic or other reproduction, translation, distribution and making publicly available.

1st edition March 2021
ISBN: 9798575915164

Authors: Adrian Langenscheid, Dr. Stefanie Gräf, M.A., Alexander Apeitos, Franziska Singer, Amrei Baumgartl, Amanda Hintz
Editing: Hannah Thier, Luise Esau, Ed Jenkins
Printing: Amazon Media EU S.á r.l., 5 Rue Plaetis, L-2338, Luxembourg
Cover picture: © Canva (canva.com)
Cover design: Pixa Heros, Stuttgart

ADRIAN LANGENSCHEID

TRUE CRIME UK

REAL CRIMINAL CASES FROM GREAT BRITAIN

About this book:

Cold-blooded murders, tragic kidnappings, vicious torture, ruthless abuse, disastrous family dramas, a stone-cold serial killer, and a millennium robbery: twenty true crime short stories from Great Britain.

Even judges, public prosecutors, and defence lawyers are not indifferent when defendants stand trial for particularly unscrupulous acts and the shocking fates of the victims and their families gradually come to light. Ideally, the final verdict ensures that the perpetrators are punished fairly - ideally.

About the author:

Adrian Langenscheid is the author of the successful book series True Crime International. His work encompasses several disciplines and is dedicated to the narration of human experiences. As a passionate True Crime expert, Adrian is named in the same breath as German True Crime giants, such as Harbort, Benecke or Tsokos, after his bestselling debut "True Crime Germany" and its successful sequel "True Crime USA". The third book in the series continued the remarkable success of its predecessors. Together with his wife and children, Adrian lives in Stuttgart, Baden Württemberg.

Table of Contents

Preface *1*

Introduction *3*

Chapter One: He doesn't breathe anymore! 7

Chapter Two: Destructive family bonds 17

Chapter Three: The Crime of the Century 29

Chapter Four: For a Drink 41

Chapter Five: The best Mum 55

Chapter Six: "Britain's most wanted man" 67

Chapter Seven: A majestic nightgown 77

Chapter Eight: Cut up faces 89

Chapter Nine: The fallen angel 101

Chapter Ten: The rope awaits her 115

Chapter Eleven: A pact among the hopeless 127

Chapter Twelve: The surrogate family 139

Chapter Thirteen: Brazilian preferences 151

Chapter Fourteen: Dangerous love affair 159

Chapter Fifteen: The Good Samaritan 171

Chapter Sixteen: A simple, white pocket watch 183

Chapter Seventeen: An immortal soul 195

Chapter Eighteen: Stumbling block for the wrong person 209

Chapter Nineteen: Fatal lies 223

Chapter Twenty: Truants 235

UK True Crime *247*

Crime Books UNLTD PODCAST *248*

True Crime International: *249*

Closing remarks by the author *251*

Preface

The year 2019 held many surprises for me. Without great expectations and out of passionate interest in True Crime, I published my first book "True Crime Germany". After that, events really took off. Within only three weeks, the debut became a bestseller, and the successor, "True Crime USA", did the same. Several months later, both books are still on the True Crime bestseller list thanks to the numerous readers. The books have been translated into English and Spanish and recorded as audio books.

This unexpected success has humbled me to this day. Without all the readers who share my interest in True Crime and leave reviews on Amazon, this would certainly not have been possible. Because only through you, dear readers, can it be possible for smaller authors who do not have large marketing budgets and publishers behind them to be found in public. With "True Crime UK" you are now listening to the third book of the series. I gratefully dedicate it to you and all those who have contributed to the success of this book series with their purchase, feedback, and reviews.

Thank you!

Adrian Langenscheid

Introduction

I am a passionate True Crime reader and love to listen to podcasts about true crimes. Most of all, I have been fascinated by re-narratives of real crimes. Oftentimes, the fates portrayed shock me and I am amazed to discover what people are capable of in my research. After countless hours, days, and weeks of True Crime, I ask myself why we humans are so fascinated by it? After all, we don't deal with fictional stories, but the unsparing reality that is linked to the unspeakable suffering of others. Is it voyeurism or the primeval human need for security? Probably both.

Motorway accidents continue to be gawked at. However, people certainly also have the basic need to better assess potentially dangerous situations so that they can do their best to prevent them. The aim is to avoid becoming the victim of such a cruel event. If it can be prevented at all. For in many of the crimes that followed, people like you and I became the victims of horrible deeds through no fault of their own.

If I had to choose a word that describes True Crime for me in essence, it would probably be the word "lost". True Crime are real life crimes from the neighbourhood. Horrible stories that life writes and that put all fiction in the shade. Something is always lost: Sometimes it is love, the mind, the feeling of security, humanity, the respect of a neighbour, an innocent life or a missed chance for a future in freedom, which got lost in the dramaturgy of life and cannot be found again.

But it is not only the victims and their loved ones who lose - the relatives of the perpetrator also mourn the loss of a father, a mother, a son, or a friend. What remains is a black hole full of remorse or shame, which in its greed to regain what has been lost devours everything in its path. Some people become depressed by the loss. Others become aggressive. The victim of yesterday sometimes becomes the perpetrator of today and the spiral of loss and quest begins again.

It is the many unanswered and unanswerable questions that leave protagonists and viewers so stunned and shocked: What if the last words to my now missing sister were not "I hate you"? Could these deeds have been prevented? And if so, who had the power to turn the terrible fate around? What if such a cruel fate had been inflicted on me? Or was it all just an irony of coincidence? Could I find hope and peace again? Is it true that under certain conditions, each of us is capable of killing a human being? What are those conditions? Are they in unspeakably deep abysses behind the bourgeois façade of acquaintances, the warm behaviour of dear friends, the nice family next door or the helpfulness of the obliging neighbour? Reading the following short stories will give you an idea. But be warned: True Crime is not for the faint of heart; the depths of the human abyss can be deeply disturbing.

In this book I present 20 criminal cases from Great Britain. Crimes that have happened in real life - and not long ago. I'm very pleased that three great German-language podcasts are included in this book. If you speak German, I highly recommend each one of them.

Let yourself be carried away by murder, extortion, torture and abuse, a spectacular kidnapping, and a sensational millennium robbery, inspired to puzzle and move you to tears! Feel the unimaginable pain of the victims and their relatives! Feel the blatant injustice, when in some cases the perpetrator cannot be identified, but an innocent man takes his place in prison and is only rehabilitated after decades. You will even meet the Queen on the following pages. Put yourself in the shoes of the people involved and be amazed at how reality outshines even the most sophisticated imagination!

Unsparingly, I present the true facts in short story form. Each case alone could fill books, but that is not my intention. Short stories are like a storm that breaks out of nowhere. Before you know it, it has left nothing but destruction in its wake. What is left behind, besides many questions, are strong emotions and a feeling for what really counts in life. It is crimes in short form that make you think further.

When reading these stories, you will laugh and cry, be amazed, horrified and speechless. Shocked, you will question everything you think you know about human nature.

Immerse yourself in the fascinating world of true crimes.

CHAPTER ONE:

He doesn't breathe anymore!

As the call arrives at 3:07 am on March 3, 2012, the service staff of the medical emergency call centre are fully concentrated as usual. This is the time when most heart attacks occur. But it soon becomes clear that this is something completely different.

On the line is a young woman with a strong Polish accent. She is distraught and slight panic resonates in her voice when she asks for an ambulance. Something bad has happened at her home. Her four-year-old son is in critical condition.

The employee immediately asks what exactly is going on with him. This information is needed and passed on to the rescue team, so that they can react more quickly. The mother than blurts out, "He doesn't breathe anymore!"

At the end of 2005, Eryk Pełka moves from Poland to Great Britain with his 27-year-old wife, Magdalena Łuczak, and their first child. The small family settles in the industrial city of Coventry in the West Midlands. On July 15 2007, little Daniel is born. Although the marriage is probably already in crisis, a third child is born. At the end of 2008, Eryk makes a momentous decision that seals the end of the marriage: He will return to Poland. His ex-wife chooses to stay in Coventry with the children.

A short time later she meets and falls in love with a Polish man, Mariusz Krężołek. A relationship with ups and downs, with suspected violence against Magdalena. This seems to have raised doubts about the safety of the children, especially little Daniel, who is at the centre of the concerns. Since November 2008, staff members of the Children, Learning and Young People Directorate (CLYP), a welfare institution for children, have been observing the family. On January 29, 2009, a social worker also paid a visit. After a thorough interview with the mother, he is convinced that Magdalena Łuczak is quite capable of adequately protecting her children.

In the following year, Mariusz Krężołek moves in with the mother of three and becomes the surrogate father of her children. Shortly afterwards, a health control employee notes in his visit that Daniel has a bruise on the side of his head. He is assured that the two-year-old boy fell off the sofa.

On August 8, 2009, the police are called. After a violent argument, the couple attacked each other with knives, causing Magdalena to suffer a small cut. Since her partner also choked her violently, the attractive woman with the sea-blue eyes and dark hair loses consciousness for a while. When she regains consciousness, she is questioned by the police about what happened. Both were drunk when the fight broke out. Magdalena also admits that her children saw everything.

Furthermore, Łuczak states that her partner downloaded child pornography onto his computer and raped her several times. Although he is arrested for the attack on Łuczak, he is released without charge. A similar case of domestic violence is recorded again on December 27,2009.

By 2011, the situation between the two partners improves, and there seem to be no further escalations. This year, however, a big step is in store for little Daniel: The little boy will be four years old and will start pre-school in the coming September. Photos show him as an extremely cute little fellow with a roundish, open face, from which bright blue eyes look mischievously back at you, and straw blond hair. He probably looks like his biological father as his mother Magdalena has dark hair.

Nevertheless, 2011 does not start well for Daniel: On January 6, his mother and Krężołek take him to the hospital with a broken arm. During the examination, the doctors discover several bruises and effusions on the arm, the left shoulder, and the child's lower abdomen. It turns out that the accident in which Daniel broke his arm was 12 hours ago. His siblings confirm the parents' story but cannot look the hospital staff in the eyes. Because the doctor finds the explanation to be credible, the youth welfare office and the social services are not involved.

Daniel is also routinely weighed - the gauge stops at 14.8 kilos. According to the report, the boy has a normal relationship with his mother and stepfather.

On September 14, Daniel will be enrolled in the preschool of Little Heath Primary School in Coventry. At this time, no one around him has any idea what the four-year-old's real life will be like. There is a reason why Magdalena and Mariusz are now so harmonious with each other. Obviously, they have found another outlet for their aggressions: Daniel. Text messages are documented for October 7, proving that he is regularly locked up in a tiny, unheated storeroom that has no door handle on the inside. Mariusz says on this day: "Put him in the room and leave him there. Then you'll get some rest." A message from Magdalena is an indication that her son often went hungry as punishment: "We will take care of Daniel when he comes home from school. He won't get any food."

In November, teachers and caregivers first notice that Daniel is stealing food from other children's lunch boxes. He also makes extremely frequent use of the "Fruit Corner" in the classroom. While his classmates usually just take one, Daniel regularly eats four to five pieces. For the teachers, everything points towards an obsession with food.

Daniel's mother Magdalena previously told doctors that Daniel robs the fridge at night and punches his stepfather if he withholds food from him. The advice of a social worker is simply to give him a little snack on his way to school. The fact that his attendance is only 63% is not registered.

An appointment with the paediatrician scheduled for November 15 will not be observed. Łuczak writes to her partner: "I will call the clinic and postpone his appointment. He is even worse off than before." On December 14, a member of staff from the Youth Welfare Office visits Daniel's family. He is told that Magdalena is not well and that she could not bring Daniel to school. Meanwhile, the boy is sitting at the kitchen table eating cornflakes.

At the beginning of 2012, the child's supposed eating obsession is getting stronger and stronger, and he begins to fish food out of the bin. He even eats half a birthday cake that a teacher had brought for the whole class. Daniel talks other children out of their food and then secretly eats it in the toilet. He digs up beans planted in the ground and eats them, too.

Meanwhile, the deputy headmaster is surprised at Daniel's lack of growth. Later, the boy's severe weight loss is also noticeable. Teachers discover fingerprints on Daniel's neck and bruises are noticed on his face again and again between December 2011 and February 2012. But nobody intervenes. The paediatrician, to whom Daniel is introduced to on February 10, 2012, cannot find anything dramatic. The boy is thin, but "not atrophied". The doctor, therefore, suspects worm infestation and prescribes an appropriate remedy.

On February 28, Daniel's face is described by the school staff as "doughy" with "sunken eyes". He also no longer interacts with his classmates. He continues his search for food in garbage cans.

One day later, on March 1, the child again picks up a half-eaten piece of fruit from the rubbish and eats "slime" that other children have played with in the sandbox. Footage from the school's security camera shows Daniel being picked up by his mother after class. These are the last moments where the four-year-old boy is seen alive.

Between 4 and 5 p.m., Daniel's long ordeal reaches its tragic climax. Because he wets himself, he is brutally beaten as punishment. His entire body is beaten black and blue. He subsequently suffers severe brain damage - and falls into a coma.

But even now, Magdalena does not react like a normal mother would by taking him to the nearest hospital. Perhaps the fear is too great that everything will come out. The next day she and her partner use Google. Based on the keywords entered, it can be reconstructed that they are looking for information about salt poisoning. At 11:25 a.m. the helpless mother enters the words "care - patient in a coma" as a search term in the search engine's query line.

Apparently, she feels on the safe side, because in the afternoon at 4:30 pm Krężołek receives several text messages; in one, the mother writes: "He will get over it." In another, she stresses that there is no reason to call an ambulance, because that would "cause real problems".

In the night, Łuczak changes her mind, presumably Daniel's condition worsens in the short term. Around 3:07 am in the early morning of March 3, she dials 999 because her child is no longer breathing. The ambulance service brings the boy, who has suffered a cardiac arrest, directly to Coventry University Hospital, where they desperately try to resuscitate him. At 3:50 a.m., Daniel Łuczak is officially declared dead.

The autopsy shook the performers severely. A total of 22 injuries were found, ten of them on the head. A resulting brain injury led to the child's death. Daniel was extremely underweight, his appearance appeared to eyewitnesses as that of a "victim from a concentration camp" or a "seriously ill cancer patient". He was completely emaciated and weighed only 10.4 kilos when he died. Hardly more than a one-year-old infant.

His mother and stepfather were arrested immediately, and investigations were started into a particularly serious case of child abuse.

For the public, the story of the unfortunate child is a real shock, the sympathy is huge. When it becomes public that the boy's biological father wants to bring the body of his son to Poland and have it buried in his hometown Łódź, but cannot pay for it, a generous supporter is found. A Polish funeral home from London donates the necessary amount, so that Daniel can finally be buried in a white child's coffin near his father on September 3, 2013. At the same time, a memorial will be erected for him at St. Paul's Cemetery in Foleshill, Coventry.

He doesn't breathe anymore!

A few months earlier, on July 31, 2013, his mother, Magdalena Łuczak, and her partner, Mariusz Krężołek, are found guilty of murder. The sentence for their unimaginable offences: at least 30 years each.

Both deny being responsible for his death but admit to cruelty towards the child. What comes to light during the trial, however, is more than just shocking; the two have systematically starved the child, locked him away in a storeroom, which Daniel also had to use as a toilet, they forcibly infused the boy with salt and used the torture method of waterboarding. Łuczak defends herself by saying that Krężołek threatened to strangle her if she protected Daniel.

The older, seven-year-old sibling is also questioned - and this time she doesn't have to lie. She says she tried to help Daniel several times. When she found some money, she went with her brother to a shop and secretly bought him food. Besides, she always had to clean the little boy. The child also reports that the mother and her partner once even tried to drown Daniel together. Krężołek had hit his head against the tub and kicked him, the mother pressed her son under water. This is evidenced by a text message and a Google search query looking for "how to get water out of the lungs". Daniel had to sleep on an old mattress soaked with urine in the hallway, but time and time again he also ended up in the small storage room, which had no door handle, so the siblings couldn't let him out. If the starving child was caught stealing food, he was force-fed salt. Other punishments included excessive knee bends.

In her reasoning for the verdict, the presiding judge expressed her dismay and described the cruelties as "extremely horrible" and the starvation as "unprecedented in this country". She further points out a deliberate and cynical deception of school, healthcare, and doctors - only to hide what was happening, so that Daniel would not get any help.

Afterwards, the case is intensively investigated by the responsible authorities. The topic was how something like this could have been overlooked - and how to reliably avoid it in the future.

The two convicts did not have to serve 30 years. On July 14, 2015, Łuczak was found lifeless in her cell at 7:15 a.m. She had hanged herself one day before what would have been Daniel's eighth birthday. On January 27, 2016, Krężołek is also found dead in his cell at 8:30 am. Heart attack. He refused medical treatment for fear that people would recognise him.

CHAPTER TWO:

Destructive family bonds

In Spring 2016, a terrible crime shocks the town of Luton. The act itself is full of brutality and cruelty, but the full implications reveal an infinite tragedy. For on the evening of May 23, a 34-year-old woman dies. She is described by neighbours and acquaintances as reserved but truly kind. The particularly tragic thing about this is that the woman is not only torn from the midst of life, but she also leaves behind four young children. These children now have to grow up without their mother, who was snatched from them by a perpetrator who stabbed her to death. But that is not even half the story.

On the evening of May 23, the semi-detached house of the Khan family on Overstone Road in Luton stands peacefully. Only the four children and Sabah are at home that evening. Sabah is Saima's 26-year-old sister, who often looks after the little ones. Since Saima still has to nurse a patient, she could not attend the funeral of an aunt in the mosque like the rest of the family. Her parents, her brother, as well as her 36-year-old husband, the taxi driver, Hafeez Rehman, attend the ceremony.

Six adults and four children have to sleep in just three bedrooms. A situation of claustrophobic confinement, where emotions inevitably boil up again and again, because it is near impossible to avoid each other. But for the Pakistani extended family, this reality is a normal situation, because family cohesion is of great importance in their culture.

The house is already dark when Saima returns from her patient visit at 11:07pm. A neighbour's surveillance camera captures her as she walks to the front door, unlocks it, and enters the house. Inside, she turns on the light - but 45 seconds later something strange happens: It suddenly becomes pitch black.

A few minutes later, desperate cries suddenly sound, wrenching the neighbours from their sleep. But the cries break off quickly and abruptly. Only to begin again with increased intensity shortly afterwards. Now, the Khan family returns from the funeral in a great hurry because they have received a strange call from Saima's sister, Sabah.

Destructive family bonds

When they enter the house and turn on the lights, they find themselves in the middle of a scene that could only be described as horrifying. On the floor, Saima lies in a pool of her own blood. It pulses inexorably from the stump of her arm, as well as from her throat and the other numerous stab wounds. Some of her clothes have been pulled off; the forensic doctors will later state that the perpetrator did this in order to ram his knife more easily and more deeply into the body after the victim's death. .

And on the floor above, her four children (two girls aged seven and one, the boys aged five and three) are lying in their beds, completely oblivious to what is unfolding downstairs.

Screaming with horror and despair, the Khans and Saima's husband Hafeez Rehman runs out. Sabah, who first discovered the dead woman, is downright hysterical. Everywhere in the neighbourhood, windows are torn open. Some come out into the street because everyone is wondering what is going on. Even the police and the ambulance are now arriving. All were also called by Sabah, right after she had informed her family. But the rescue services can do nothing more for the woman. At 11:30 pm, Saima is declared dead.

The animalistic savagery of the murder appals both the rescue workers and the officers of the British police.

The corpse is covered with stab wounds - later it turns out that the murderer must have stabbed Saima in a blind bloodlust, because after 68 stab wounds the examining pathologists stop counting. Simply because, with the body butchered, they can no longer tell where one stab wound ends, and where another begins. A hand was cut off and many things point to the attempt of cutting off the head as well.

Gradually, the detectives begin the first round of interrogations. They concentrate mainly on Sabah, who was the one to find her sister. Although she is still completely upset, she tries hard to answer the questions. She had just been in the shower when the back door was ripped open, so she was hiding in fear. Apparently, burglars had entered the house, who were surprised by Saima and therefore panicked. Sabah goes on to say that she tried to save her sister's life.

In fact, there are traces found in the house that support the robbery story: Windows smashed, bedrooms ransacked, jewellery missing.

When the interrogating officer asks Sabah about the blood on her arm, she tells him that she cut herself on the broken glass from the window.

Over the next few days, the police investigate in all directions. Although they are checking the burglary theory, a so-called "honour murder" is not ruled out either. But early on in the investigation, the impression is created that everything does not seem to be fitting together. Saima's children are also questioned. The three younger ones were sound asleep during the crime, only the older daughter was awake. She says that she was awakened by a noise. First, she thought it was her aunt and called downstairs: "Auntie, are you killing a mouse?" - the girl received only the harsh reply, "Don't come down."

For the inhabitants of Luton, the days after the murder are marked by horror and suspicion. Who goes about their town killing women who wouldn't harm a fly? Who takes the mother of four small children in such a heartless manner?

Just one week later, an arrest in the Saima Khan case is made. The news that a 26-year-old woman has been arrested for the murder comes as shock to all. In the bedroom of the arrested woman, an investigator finds a black garbage bag with bloodstained clothes, a knife, and gloves. There is blood on these as well. The blood of Saima Khan, as the forensic investigation will later reveal. Forensics found tiny glass splinters on the clothing. Window glass. That is, the perpetrator personally and deliberately destroyed the window to set up a false trail. Furthermore, recordings of a surveillance camera show that the suspect bought the murder weapon in a local shop only a few days before the murder. The pieces of the puzzle quickly fall into place and everything points to this one person. The arrested person denies the crime and is apparently shocked by the accusations. And she affirms that she has always loved her sister! The suspect is Sabah Khan.

But how can that be? - This is the question that keeps coming up. Stunned, people try to understand how a younger sister could possibly develop such hatred. A hatred so strong that one is capable of murdering their own sister. At the arrest, the police also confiscated Sabah's smartphone. During the subsequent search of the data, it becomes clearer how this incredible, monstrous betrayal of her own sister and her family came about.

In October 2017, the trial will begin in London's Old Bailey Court, presided over by Judge Christopher Moss. It quickly becomes clear that the reason for the murder was pure jealousy. Jealousy of Saima's life - or more precisely of her husband and children. And ultimately, perhaps horror at the fact that her sister was planning to leave her, Sabah, behind.

The trigger for the atrocity of May 23rd is an affair that Sabah starts in 2012 with Saima's husband, Hafeez Rehman. Did Saima have no idea about all this or did she simply prefer to pretend not to notice? The love affair begins shortly after the birth of Saima's second baby; after several rejections from Hafeez. To have sex, they use the back seat of his taxi. The dalliance even goes so far that Sabah becomes pregnant by her brother-in-law; however, she has the child aborted.

Their relationship turns out to be highly emotional - at least for Sabah, who is desperately fighting for the man of her dreams. She is jealous of her sister and wants him all to herself. She reproaches him several times via WhatsApp. Her sister always calls her a "bitch". Sabah accuses Hafeez Rehman of having married her sister only because of a residence permit. In a message she also complains: "With the bitch you text 24/7, all day long, but you don't have time for me!" The husband and father later tells the police that he wanted to end the affair, but that she threatened to harm herself. Sabah wrote to her lover: "Nothing in the world can change my feelings for you, not even you; no matter how badly you treat me, it will not change anything. Day by day my love grows stronger."

At some point, Hafeez blocks his sister-in-law on WhatsApp. He had previously inquired whether Islam allows for both sisters to marry at the same time. During the trial, Saima's husband tries hard to portray his sister-in-law as the one who seduced him into the affair. But the text messages certainly suggest another version.

It is unclear exactly why the turnaround is coming. But at some point, Sabah must realise that Hafeez Rehman will not leave her older sister for her. This is probably the moment when she begins searching the internet for ways of killing without leaving any traces. About three months before the murder, she informs herself about poisonous snakes and surfs the website "16 steps to kill everyone without getting caught". She also contacts a black magician in Pakistan, who is supposed to bewitch and kill her sister. For this she even transfers 5,000 pounds in advance, with which the man disappears without a trace.

But the younger sister only starts to get serious about the murder plans when she learns that Saima and her unfaithful husband are about to move out of the house. Does it occur to her at that moment that her sister might be taking her husband away from her? And so, an insidious plan takes shape in Sabah and the funeral of her aunt seems to be the perfect opportunity for her to put her resolution into action. The evening before, as a precaution, she informs herself on the Internet how long a Muslim funeral will take, so that she can better estimate the time frame.

Shortly after 10:00 p.m., the victim leaves the common house to look after a patient. During this time, Sabah sends her a total of four text messages in which she writes that the one-year-old girl is crying and needs her mother. She ends by telling Saima to come home quickly. Her reply: "I'm on my way".

The surveillance camera footage at a neighbouring house then shows Saima opening the door of the family home at 11:07 p.m. and turning on the lights in the hallway. 45 seconds later, the lights go out - and only after eight minutes do they come on again.

During these eight minutes, Sabah brutally slaughters her older sister. She ambushes Saima in the hallway. In her hand she holds the large kitchen knife. She turns off the light, jumps out of her hiding place, and stabs her totally surprised sister again and again with an almost insane ferocity. The cut above the throat is made with such force that it almost cuts her head off. Saima's desperate cries can be heard miles away before she finally sinks to the ground. Whether Sabah cuts off the hand because the murder guidebook on the website "16 steps ..." recommends such a thing, is unclear.

The noise wakes up Saima's seven-year-old daughter, who asks what is going on. Sabah orders her not to come down. She then smashes the window of the back door, stuffs the knife and the black, bloodstained clothes into the garbage bag and hides it in her bedroom. At 11:25 pm, she calls her parents and tries to make everything look like a failed break-in.

After this shocking murder reconstruction, Sabah Khan's defence attorney has a hard time coming up with exculpatory evidence for his client. It becomes apparent how this immeasurably deep jealousy and the subsequent excess of violence could have come about in the first place. He points out that she is a very lonely person who suffers from psychological problems. Sabah has been displaying self-harming behaviour for some time now; she has cut herself and even choked herself. A psychiatric report read out during the trial confirms that the 26-year-old is emotionally unstable and suffers from some form of depressive disorder. Was she therefore unable to control her nagging jealousy? Psychologist, Emma Kenny's, explanation points in that direction. She assumes that Sabah had to commit the murder in her imagination. Since her brother-in-law would not part with her sister and they wanted to move out, she would lose both her lover and her sister. And that would have caused this enormous blind rage.

Sabah Khan pleaded innocent at the beginning of the trial, but after the revelations, the burden of proof is too heavy. She finally pleads guilty - and accepts the judgement without any emotion. The sentence is: at least 22 years imprisonment. Sabah loses not only her life in freedom, but also her family and the love of her life.

Hafeez Rehman, the father, widower, and lover, is very shocked by the events during the investigation and also during the trial. He emphasises that he would now take more care of his four children - although he could never replace the loving mother, of course. In an interview shortly afterwards, he will say: "She was a loving mother of four beautiful children, a devoted wife, a beloved daughter and the most caring of all sisters.

About a year after the murder, the family sell the house in Overstone Road. The purchase price for the crime scene with the three bedrooms is £360,000.

CHAPTER THREE:

The Crime of the Century

The board game Monopoly is a real classic, but how about playing with real notes instead of colourful play money? With hundreds, thousands, or even bigger banknotes? In August 1963, this dream became reality for at least 15 men. One of the reasons why "The Great Train Robbery" became a legend. But it's also this Monopoly passion that finally provides the police with valuable information about a case that has been setting standards in the history of crime for over 50 years.

1963 is a special year: it begins with the reconciliation of Germany and France and the historic signing of the Élysée Treaty by Charles de Gaulle and Konrad Adenauer. In February, the Shah introduces the right to vote for women in Iran. On June 26, US President John F. Kennedy ends his famous speech in the divided German capital with the words: "I am a Berliner."

And, in England, Ronald Biggs calls his partner in crime, Bruce Reynolds (32), wanting to borrow 500 pounds from him. His answer is surprising. Unfortunately, he cannot lend him the money, but he would like to talk to him in person.

At this time, Reynolds, who has worked his way up from minor crimes to the upper class of criminals (including amenities like holidays on the Côte d'Azur and cars of the noble brand Aston Martin), is just about to gather a gang of secretive and reliable men around him. In his memoirs, Reynolds confesses about this time: "I began to see the thief as an artist, an artist who writes the script, chooses the actors and the location, directs and plays along with them". Perhaps this is also how he gets the idea for his next coup. A production with which he wants to surpass himself as a directing artist.

Reynolds plans the raid with general staff; later on, he is even occasionally offered a military career in the Royal Army. In the end, he has a gang of at least 15 - men who dream of big money and a life of luxury. On board are Ronald Biggs, Buster Edwards, Roger Cordrey and John Daly, as well as Gordon Goody, Jimmy Hussey, Roy James, Robert Welch, Jimmy White, Charlie Wilson, and

Tommy Wisbey; most likely three more people will join them. Lovingly, Reynolds later calls these men the "veteran meeting of the country's elite criminals". And as befits the criminal elite, the esteemed gentlemen of crime also have their own code of honour. Their ironclad principle is "no one will snitch." Additionally, Reynolds prefers, for safety's sake, that none of the men know the complete plan and a strict ban on talking to relatives is imposed.

The spectacular raid is planned for August 7, 1963, but it is postponed for a day when Reynolds finds out that on August 8, the loot will be even more lucrative.

At this time, British banks are having several million pounds transported by train through Britain every day. They use the regular mail trains that travel across the country at night to deliver letters, parcels, and packages to their recipients. Security guards are on duty to ensure the safety of the money bags. A perfect match for the clever Reynolds, who likes to pose in photos as a gentleman in fine tweed, with silver rimmed glasses and a mischievous smile.

It is August 8, 1963, and at 6:50 p.m. the mail train to London leaves Glasgow station right on schedule. On board are 128 bags of cash, totalling more than 2.6 million pounds (today's purchasing power: around 58 million euros). This enormous sum is guarded by just five postal workers. Behind the locomotive hangs an unmanned parcel wagon, then follows the wagon with the cash; behind it comes the wagons with the mail sorters.

Early in the morning, around three o'clock, the train finally crosses Buckinghamshire County - where it is eagerly awaited! Close to the village of Cheddington, Roger Cordrey stands by at the "Sears Crossing" stop signal. When the men finally hear the fine whirring of the tracks, Cordrey takes the old glove and carefully puts it over the green signal, which is supposed to show the train that it is free to move. Then Cordrey takes a battery and holds it against the red signal, which then lights up. Suddenly, the rattling of the wheels of the approaching train come to a stop. It is shortly after 3 a.m.

While engine driver John Mills brings the train to a halt, his stoker wants to ask at the next station what's going on. But before he can use the track telephone, three men wearing helmets and ski masks suddenly push into the locomotive and overpower them. John Mills puts up a fight. To put him out of action, one of the attackers hits him over the head with an iron bar. Mills is knocked unconscious, blood running from a deep gash on his skull. But apart from that, no one is harmed - this will also contribute to the legend of the great mail robbery later on.

More robbers will take care of the rest now. First, the locomotive and the first two wagons are stripped. Then everything depends on the retired train driver, who the gang has hired and brought along especially for this purpose. But he can't cope with this modern diesel locomotive. Is this the end of the line? The robbers make a decision: they shake the unconscious train driver awake, then force him to drive the locomotive 1,200 meters further to the Bridego bridge.

While the locomotive and the first two wagons disappear, 50 postal workers in the remaining wagons are still calmly sorting letters and parcels, without the slightest hint.

Under the Bridego Bridge, a small stone bridge, there is a country road with hardly any traffic and the next houses are far away. Here, the remaining crooks are already waiting impatiently. In order for the train to stop at the right place, two men with a big, bright tarpaulin are waiting on the tracks. Finally, the locomotive comes to a halt and the remaining mail robbers act.

And they have real luck! Normally, a special high-security wagon is used for transporting money, but this evening, for once, it is in the repair shop. So, the crooks only have to break a simple lock to get at the money bags.

The human chain from the train to the transport and escape vehicles (a truck as well as two Land Rovers) has already been formed, now the gangsters start unloading the money wagon. The time window calculated for this is only 15 minutes. And it's crucial for the rest of the plan that they stick to it meticulously! The mail robbers unload about 2.5 tons of cash from the wagon. Within the tight time limit, they stow more than 100 bulging money bags in the escape vehicles. The stoker is ordered to wait at least another 30 minutes before sounding the alarm. By then, the robbery is over and the robbers hurry to get into the cars.

Now, they rush to a farm 43 kilometres away near the town of Oakley. The gangsters had rented the farm through a straw man and took up quarters here a few days ago. The hiding place was perfectly chosen: The Leatherslade farm is far enough from the crime scene not to be searched directly, but close enough to be reached before the police set up roadblocks.

Reynolds has also made sure that all telephone lines in the area are cut in advance. This is a clever move, because the very first report of the robbery is not transmitted over the police radio until around 4:30 am. A policeman from Buckinghamshire County begins his message to his colleagues with the legendary words: *"You won't believe this, but they've just stolen a train".*

Reynolds and his team stay on the Leatherslade farm for two more days before they gradually disappear. During that time, the men are in a frenzy. When they arrive at the farm, the stolen money is spread over the ground. One of the cunning crooks even dances euphorically around the loot and sings along. The gangsters now gamble with real bills until they leave the farm one by one. The last remaining gang member is ordered by Reynolds to burn down the farm to remove any traces. But here of all places the first indiscipline occurs, which will have serious consequences. It remains unclear why the last gangster, whose name is still unknown, does not carry out this order. Does he perhaps simply consider it unnecessary, because in his euphoria he considers himself untouchable? Or did he think that time was running out because the police were increasingly closing in on them?

The police started with a wide-ranging manhunt as soon as they became aware of the robbery. Virtually every house is searched, every citizen questioned, every stone turned. The public is urged to help. On almost every route, roadblocks are set up and everyone who wants to pass through them is searched intensively. And even though the robbery was carried out with the utmost care and attention to the smallest detail, Scotland Yard finally gets the gangsters into trouble relatively quickly. The decisive clue for Chief Inspector Malcolm Fewtrell is the gangsters' instruction that the stoker and train driver are not allowed to sound the alarm for at least half an hour. From this the investigator concludes that the hiding place must be within a radius of 30 miles (just under 50 kilometres). This allows Fewtrell to narrow the search radius considerably. When a high reward is finally offered for clues, the first important tip is quickly given: A cattle owner from Oakley makes a report on August 13 and points out the new inhabitants of the Leatherslade farm. A red-hot lead, as the local police officers soon realise. Because here they discover not only the escape vehicles used for the robbery, but also mail sacks, banderols of bank note packages and lots of fingerprints. For while the perpetrators wore gloves in the house around the clock before the robbery, 15 of them disregarded this precaution after the robbery.

Just one day later, on August 14, the police already have the first two perpetrators in the net. They try to rent a garage, possibly to hide their loot, utensils, and maybe even themselves for a while. However, the two don't suspect that they are going to present themselves to a police widow, who is currently offering a garage for rent. She knows that the perpetrators of the mail train robbery are fugitives, and through her late husband she has gained enough insight into police work that she immediately becomes suspicious of them. She informs the police and the two are arrested. And even until most of the remaining gangsters are caught, only a few months pass by. Even the straw men John Wheater, Leonard Field and Brian Field, who bought the shelter on behalf of the robbers, are tracked down. Only the head of the gang, Bruce Reynolds, manages to go into hiding and escape to Mexico.

What the authorities don't realise for the time being is the admiration that the brilliant coup arouses in the population. For many, the robbers are real heroes, because the almost complete renunciation of violence and the extraordinarily disciplined execution quickly gives rise to the modern legend of the gentleman robbers. And also, the ingenuity with regard to the consequent planning down to the smallest details arouses admiration everywhere.

But from an official point of view, they want to take rigorous action against the men who, with an almost impudent nonchalance, have led both banks and post offices and the police by the nose. For this reason, the longest trial in British judicial history to date begins on January 20 1964 in Aylesbury under the presidency of Judge Edmund Davies - three months will pass before the verdict is reached. It is clear from the outset that an example is to be set. In this respect, it is not being investigated exactly whether all the accused men were actually involved in the attack and what role they had assumed. This leads to misjudgements. Two of the condemned men are most likely innocent. Other persons involved, however, are never found and brought to trial, such as the retired train driver.

Biggs, Goody, Hussey, James, Welch, Wilson and Wisbey are sentenced to 30 years in prison. This means that they will be punished more severely than criminals who have committed child murder or rape. Boal and Cordrey get 14 years, Brian and Leonard Field 5 years each and Wheater 3 years in prison. Only John Daly is acquitted because there is not enough evidence against him.

In the grounds for his verdict, Judge Davies explains why he is using the full force of the law: "You and your co-defendants have been convicted of participation in a crime that is unprecedented in its audacity and enormity in this century. I will do everything in my power to see that it remains the last."

But the irony of the story is that, with his draconian intervention, the judge only achieves the exact opposite. For the extremely severe sentence will trigger a reform of the criminal law in Great Britain, which will release the main culprits back to freedom after only a decade of incarceration.

However, some of the imprisoned mail robbers will not remain idle. Already on August 12, 1964 Charlie Wilson manages to escape from prison near Birmingham with the help of unknown persons. He flees via Mexico to Canada, where Scotland Yard is able to track him down again in 1968 near Montreal - because his wife calls relatives in England. However, ten years later he is already released again.

On July 8, 1965, Ronald Biggs escapes from Wandsworth Prison in South London. Several armed and masked men lower a rope ladder from a lifting platform over the prison wall so that Biggs and three other inmates can escape. After a long flight across the continents, Biggs finally lands in Brazil, where he gains a foothold in Rio de Janeiro. When Scotland Yard tracks him down there in 1973, the arrest fails because Biggs has a son with his Brazilian mistress and therefore cannot be extradited. Thus, the game of hide-and-seek also ends, and he quickly becomes a kind of "crime pop star". However, he is financially on the brink of destitution, so he uses his fame to make music with the Sex Pistols as well as the Dead Pants and tells holidaymakers the story of the big raid during a barbecue at his home for a fee. In 2001, Biggs also returned to his home country, England, where he was arrested by return of post; he was not pardoned until 2009. Four years later he dies at the age of 84.

Bruce Reynolds, the leader of the gang, returns unrecognised from Mexico to the British Isles, where he is arrested in 1968 in a rented villa by the sea. He is released in 1978 but has problems with a thoroughly respectable life. Reynolds dies in 2013.

The big question that still occupies everyone's mind is: Where did all the stolen money go? - a whopping 2,631,684 British pounds. The robbers divided the catch, which mainly consisted of small notes, into 16 or 17 equal parts, i.e. about 150,000 pounds per person. Only 340,000 pounds can be traced by the police, the rest disappeared without a trace.

When a journalist asks Biggs in an interview shortly before his death whether he regrets having taken part in the coup that kept him on the run and in prison for so long, he only replies: "I am even proud to have been one of them. What counts is that I was there that night in August. I am one of the few witnesses of this crime of the century."

CHAPTER FOUR:

For a Drink
(by Franziska Singer / "Darf's ein bisserl Mord sein?")

Dennis Andrew Nilsen was born on November 23, 1945, in the Aberdeen area of north-east Scotland. He is the second of three children of Elizabeth Whyte and the Norwegian Olav Moksheim, who had taken the name Nilsen. Dennis' father fights in the Norwegian resistance against the Nazis and is more interested in alcohol than family life. Soon after the birth of their third child together, Dennis' parents' divorce.

Young Dennis spends a lot of time with his grandfather, Andrew Whyte, a fisherman. He looks up to him, seeing him as his great hero and protector. When the grandfather is at sea, the child waits for him longingly. In 1951, the grandfather dies of a heart attack while at sea. His mother shows Dennis the body without preparing him for it. She tells him that the grandfather was only sleeping. The sight of the corpse causes a great emotional trauma for the six-year-old, which will have lasting effects on him and on the way he thinks.

When Dennis is eight years old, he is playing alone by the sea as he often does and is suddenly caught by a wave. He almost drowns, but another boy saves him. This is also a particularly memorable moment for him.

Two years later his mother marries a new man and has four more children. She has no more time for Dennis and his two direct siblings. So, Dennis becomes a quiet loner. He never tortures small animals or other children as some boys do, on the contrary: he cannot stand violence. He also slowly realises that he is not particularly interested in girls, but more in other boys. Nevertheless, or perhaps just to put this to the test, he first gropes his sister and then his brother in their sleep.

In 1961, at the age of 16, Dennis joins the British Army. For the first three years, the teenager is stationed in Aldershot, a town about 50 kilometres southwest of London. There Dennis trains as an army cook and learns how to slaughter animals. Because of his homosexuality, which is still a criminal offence in the sixties, he tends to stay away from his comrades. Then, in 1963, the young man is stationed in Osnabrück, later in Norway, and finally in Aden (today South Yemen), where he sees some of his colleagues die in surprise attacks. Already during his time in Germany Dennis begins to get drunk more and more often and his sexual fantasies develop strongly in a certain direction. Either he or the other person should be unconscious during sex. Nilsen, for example, pretends several times to fall asleep, drunk as a skunk, with his pants slightly down, in the hope that someone will take advantage of his body. Or, when he is alone, he lies down in front of a mirror so that he cannot see his own head. The sight of this "unconscious body" excites him so much that he masturbates to it. One of these fantasies, which he will talk about later, looks like this: A slim, young soldier who has recently died in battle is washed by a faceless, "dirty, grey-haired old man" before the man consorts with the corpse. This fantasy is also the reason for later theories that Dennis' grandfather may have taken advantage of the boy.

Nilsen is still stationed in several places and has intercourse with a female prostitute for the first time in Berlin - he calls this experience "overrated" and "depressing".

He ends his military service in 1972. During a visit to his strictly Catholic family, he is outed as a homosexual by his brother Olav Jr.. From then on, he only maintains sporadic correspondence with his family.

Nilsen starts training as a policeman, but the most fascinating thing for him is that he can look at dead bodies in the morgue. He lacks the camaraderie of the army. After only one year he quits his job and starts working in a London employment office. Nilsen visits gay bars and occasionally gets involved in one-night stands. However, he would like a firm relationship. He describes casual sex as "soul-destroying" and "a futile search for inner peace".

One day he takes a young man he meets at the job centre home with him, where the stranger falls asleep. Nilsen takes the opportunity to take photos of him. However, the young man wakes up and runs away, falling over and injuring himself, having to go to hospital. Nilsen is questioned by the police about this incident but is released immediately.

His sexual fantasies in front of the mirror become more extreme. He uses make-up and artificial blood to create the illusion of a murdered body; and he imagines someone coming to bury him. He also includes the painting "The Raft of Medusa" by Théodore Géricault in his masturbation fantasies. In this painting, which was inspired by a real shipwreck, in which cannibalism also occurred, the muscular bodies of men pile up to form a pyramid, death and despair reign.

For a Drink

In 1975, Nilsen moved into an apartment with a man named David Gallichan at 195 Melrose Avenue. Gallichan denies any sexual activity between the two, but Nilsen calls him his first boyfriend. They have a dog and a cat together. After two years, Gallichan moves out again because the two can't stand each other anymore. Nilsen now grabs the bottle even more often than before, and becomes involved in some short-lived relationships, but none of his lovers want to move in with him or be with him for the long term.

On December 30, 1978, Dennis Nilsen is now 33 years old, he takes 14-year-old Stephen Holmes home with him. They drink alcohol and listen to music, and then they fall asleep. When Nilsen wakes up, the sight of the sleeping boy excites him. The thought that he, too, will leave him when he wakes up kills him. He has already had to spend Christmas alone; he doesn't want to be lonely at the turn of the year. And he thinks, "You're staying with me for New Year's Eve whether you want to or not." Nilsen picks up a tie from the floor and begins to strangle the boy with it. When that's not enough to kill him, he drowns him in a bucket of water. Finally, he carries Holmes into the bathroom to wash the body. He then carefully dries it and puts it back in his bed. Nilsen doesn't quite know what to do with it - he doesn't like the idea of cutting it up, so he makes himself something to eat and watches TV before deciding to bury the boy under the boards of his floor.

He said, "I put him in his new bed under the floorboards. A week later, I wondered if the condition of his body had remained the same or if he had begun to decay. I dug him up again and pulled the filthy young man up to the floor. His skin was very dirty. I stripped him naked, carried him into the bathroom and washed him. There was practically no discoloration, his skin was very pale. His limbs seemed more relaxed than when I put him down there."

Nilsen masturbates twice on the corpse and keeps it in his living room for a while before putting it back under the floorboards. Almost eight months later, he exhumed it again and burned the body in his garden. He masks the smell by simultaneously throwing a car tire into the fire.

In October 1979, Nilsen lures the Chinese student Andrew Ho to his home with the prospect of sex and then tries to strangle him. Ho runs away and reports the incident to the police but doesn't denounce him.

Two months later, Nilsen brings the Canadian tourist Kenneth Ockenden to his apartment. They drink large amounts of alcohol and listen to music together. Nilsen cannot bear the thought that his new friend will leave him the next day to fly home. Therefore, he strangles him

For a Drink

with the cable of the headphones he is wearing to listen to music. Then he pours himself another glass and puts the headphones on himself to listen to a little music before washing the dead Kenneth and putting him in his bed. The next day Nilsen stuffs the Canadian's body into his wardrobe and goes to work as normal. After work, he takes some photos of Kenneth's body and molests it before he puts it under the floorboards. Over the next few weeks, he takes Kenneth out again and puts him in a chair to watch TV with him.

In May 1980, homeless 16-year-old Martyn Duffey accepts Nilsen's invitation to cook him some food and give him a bed for the night. Like his first victim, Martyn is also strangled by Nilsen and then drowned. The body remains in Nilsen's wardrobe for two weeks before it, too, is deposited under the floorboards.

A few weeks later, Douglas Stewart wakes up after a night of drinking with Nilsen, partially tied up in an armchair - just as Nilsen begins to strangle him. Stewart knocks Nilsen down and calls the police. But the police leave again, thinking the affair is just a "quarrel among gays". Also, Stewart does not pursue the matter further.

Nilsen's next victims who do not escape him are Billy Sutherland (27) and six or seven other unidentified men between 18 and 30 years.

In September 1981, 24-year-old Malcolm Barlow suffers an epileptic seizure in front of Nilsen's house, and he calls the ambulance service. The next day Barlow comes back to thank his rescuer, he stays for a drink. Then he is murdered.

Nilsen's approach is always the same: He brings a young man to his home, often from a pub, with the prospect of more alcohol and/or an overnight stay. The young men often have no relatives or sometimes are hiding from the police. Then Nilsen either strangles his guest until he dies or drowns him if the strangling only rendered him unconscious. Afterwards, the murderer baths the dead body, dresses it again, and puts it into his bed. Nilsen leaves some of the corpses in his bed with him for a good week to use them for his sexual pleasure. He likes to have control over these men, and the fact that a dead body can no longer react exerts a strong fascination on him. Nilsen will later say that he appreciates these men more than they have ever been appreciated by anyone.

Since not all of the victims have room under the floorboards of his apartment, Nilsen cuts them up in his kitchen from a certain point on. He boils some heads in a large pot and packs the internal organs in plastic bags. He puts some of the split upper bodies into suitcases. Now and then Nilsen burns some of the body parts in his

For a Drink

garden - always at the same time as car tyres to cover up the smell. Twice a day he sprays insecticides all over his apartment to get rid of the flies. Neighbours complain about the unpleasant smell, but Nilsen blames it on the dilapidated condition of the building.

In summer 1981, Nilsen must move out because the building is to be renovated. His new flat in 23D Cranley Gardens (Muswell Hills) is on the top floor and he has no garden at his disposal.

19-year-old Paul Nobbs wakes up in Nilsen's new apartment after a night of drinking, with severe headaches and bloodshot eyes. He later has himself examined by a doctor and finds out that he must have been strangled - but he does not report Nilsen.

His next victim, John Howlett (23), also knows Nilsen from the pub. The two men have already had a good chat there several times before. One night, John accompanies Nilsen home to continue drinking there. He lies down in his bed and is attacked. John defends himself, also trying to strangle Nilsen, and although he does well, he loses the fight. Finally, he drowns, like many others before him. Nilsen still carries visible marks on his own neck for days. He cuts John into small pieces, which he flushes down the toilet. Head, hands, and feet, among other parts, he boils out. He throws some of the bones into the garbage, some larger ones into the compost, and others he puts in salt in a kitchen drawer.

New Year's Eve, 1981, Toshimitsu Ozawa goes home with Nilsen, but he gets scared and runs away when Nilsen approaches him with a tie in his hands. There are no further investigations here either.

Nilsen's next nightly visitor is Carl Stottor (21). The serial killer chokes him, but Carl wakes up. So, Nilsen sticks his head in a bucket of water. But Carl only faints. When he wakes up, he's sitting in an armchair. Nilsen is completely surprised that he is not dead, and he tells him a confused story about how he got so caught in the sleeping bag's zipper while he slept, that he almost suffocated. To revive Stottor, he dipped him in cold water. Nilsen lets Stottor go home.

The next victim is Graham Allen (27). Like some others before him, Nilsen doesn't remember having murdered him - when he regains consciousness from a "murderous trance", a corpse sits in his armchair. Allen stays in the bathtub for 3 days before Nilsen finally cuts him up.

In January 1983, the now 38-year-old Nilsen kills for the last time, the 20-year-old Stephen Sinclair. He treats him in the same way as the two other victims before him.

In February 1983, the complaints of the residents of Nilsen's house about blocked toilet drains become more and more frequent. The plumber, who comes to get an idea of the situation, finds not only a terrible stench, but also a fleshy substance and several pieces of bone within the house's drainpipe. Nilsen tells him that he thinks someone washed down food from Kentucky Fried Chicken. At night he takes the precaution of emptying the pipe. When the plumber returns the next day to clean the drain, he finds it already cleaned. But further up the pipe that leads to Nilsen's apartment, he finds a few more pieces of meat and bones. He alerts the police, who confirm the suspicion that these pieces are of human origin.

When Nilsen comes home from work, the police are there waiting for him. They gain access to his apartment, where the smell of decomposition immediately strikes them. Nilsen at first acts surprised, but soon admits that he has more body parts in his cupboard. During a search of his apartment, police officers find several bags of human remains in various stages of decomposition. When the police take Nilsen away, one of the men asks him whether the remains in his apartment belong to one or two people. Nilsen replies: "Fifteen or sixteen, since 1978." Nilsen confessed.

He makes a full confession but shows no remorse. He helps the policemen out of memory to assemble the parts that belong together and tells them everything about his first apartment and the garden. About cutting up the corpses, Nilsen says: "The victim is the dirty plate after the feast, and washing up is an ordinary, clinical act." He also says he would have gone on like this forever if they hadn't caught him.

Paul Nobbs, Douglas Stewart, and Carl Stotter will testify against Nilsen in court. A psychiatrist certifies that he has some kind of narcissistic personality disorder with schizoid outbursts, which he can keep under control most of the time. Another expert, however, says that Nilsen is just very manipulative - abnormal, yes, but he has no personality disorder.

In 1983, Dennis Nilsen is accused of murder in six cases and attempted murder in two cases and sentenced to life imprisonment. This means for him that he must remain in prison for at least 25 years.

By the way, his first victim, Stephen Holmes, is not identified until 2006 - only then Nilsen allegedly recognises him on a photo that the police show him. It is the picture of a missing boy. Since a conviction in this case would not extend the prison sentence, and the bone fragments from his first apartment have already been destroyed, Nilsen is not charged with the murder of 14-year-old Stephen Dean Holmes.

While in prison, he writes his autobiography, "History of a Drowning Boy", which has not found a publisher.

For a Drink

On May 12, 2018, Dennis Nilsen dies at the age of 72 of a pulmonary embolism, in the high security prison, Full Sutton, in Yorkshire.

In a written statement from 1983, Nielsen says: "When I am under pressure from work, when social loneliness is particularly painful and I feel completely miserable, I feel compelled to temporarily escape reality. I achieve this through large amounts of alcohol and by turning on music that mentally takes me to a place of ecstasy, happiness, and tears. This is a very emotional experience... I relive moments from my childhood to the present day, but without the bad sides. When I drink alcohol, I feel drawn out of my isolated, prison-like apartment. I bring people with me who are not always allowed to leave, because I want to share my experiences and this exhilaration with them".

CHAPTER FIVE:

The best Mum

The year 2008 is not a good year for the Matthews family from Dewsbury, West Yorkshire. Nine-year-old Shannon Louise Matthews is a happy child, even though her life circumstances are quite complicated. The cute girl with the round face and bright brown eyes that peeked out from under her fringe is still too young to be interested in the chart hits of Rihanna, Coldplay, Pink or Kid Rock. Perhaps she dreams, like other girls, of her own pony, dressing up as a princess, or watching "Madagascar 2" in the cinema. She loves dogs. Shannon comes from a lower-class family, as is common in the Yorkshire region. The unemployment rate here is around 5.9 percent - a whole percentage point higher than the national average. On the other hand, the average annual salary of people who have a job is considerably lower - namely £4000 less. Shannon's mother, 32-year-old

Karen Matthews, lives on welfare benefits and has been dreaming for some time now of having better fortune and leading a rich, carefree life. But the reality couldn't be more different: She is the mother of seven children from five different fathers. The youngest comes from her current boyfriend Craig Meehan; the 22-year-old man works as a supermarket fishmonger. Karen's parents are unhappy about the relationship, they feel that Karen has changed since then.

The fact is, however, that despite their low income, the two of them do indulge themselves in life. In their shared apartment there are three computers and also a widescreen TV.

But what nobody suspects yet, on February 19, 2008 something is supposed to happen that will turn life in Dewsbury upside down completely and create a media interest beyond the borders of Great Britain. For almost four weeks there will be a state of emergency in the city - and it all begins on that day with a phone call at 6:48 pm.

Shannon has her usual swimming lessons at Westmoor Primary School until 3pm that afternoon. The school is just half a mile, a good 800 metres, from her home, which is why she is making her own way home. At 3:10 pm she is seen for the last time in front of the school. It takes Shannon about twenty minutes to get home - but she does not arrive! Maybe she met up with a friend and went to her home? Around 6:48 pm, Karen calls the West Yorkshire police and reports the nine-year-old as missing.

The news spreads like wildfire because Matthews has first checked with everyone her daughter might be staying with. They in turn pass it on - hoping to track down Shannon. Everyone hopes and prays that Shannon has not become the victim of a child molester!

The search action, which is now starting immediately, is unparalleled: It will cost the police around 3.2 million pounds. And the population is also eager to help the search, doing its utmost to help find the child and comforting the desperate mother. All West Yorkshire suffers with her, because the thought that the little girl might have been the victim of a crime is unbearable for all parents. Heaven and hell are being blasted about, trying to find the girl. More than 200 police officers are on duty - about 1,500 car, truck and motorcycle drivers are questioned, and a total of 3,000 houses are searched. Hundreds of neighbours are also supporting the search and combing through the surrounding forests and fields. When the search remains fruitless even after 14 days, the police force is increased on March 5. This is also a reaction to the increasing public desperation, suffering, and the grief of the mother. The police officers are in a similar situation, and in this respect the increased search effort has their full support. Now, 250 officers and 60 detectives are searching for Shannon. Even 16 search dogs are in use - although there are only 27 in the whole of Great Britain in 2008. The police have also launched two websites asking for help. Everyone knows that time is running out. It has been proven that the more time passes, the less likely it is to find a child alive and unharmed.

The whole of Britain is enthralled. The media, especially the tabloids, are reporting in detail on the case, possibly under the impression of the kidnapping of little Madeleine McCann in Portugal, who also disappeared without trace. In this case, everyone is still hoping for a happy ending. Karen is repeatedly asked for interviews and statements, there is hardly a newspaper or TV station where she is not present. Oftentimes, her partner, Craig, is present. The appearances of the desperate mother with appeals to the kidnappers are touching. She begs that she be given back her beloved girl; she even prays publicly that Shannon should reappear safe and sound. These pictures move the British very much - although it is also pointed out that the lower-class mum, with seven children from five different fathers, is unfortunately not able to present herself as well as the wealthy McCanns.

Nevertheless, the public willingness to help is unbroken: The newspaper, "The Sun" is offering a £20,000 reward for information leading to Shannon's safe return home. On March 10, when the little girl has already been missing for 20 days, the amount is increased to a sensational £50,000. A company in Huddersfield, just a short distance from Dewsbury, also offers £5,000 as a reward. No-one suspects at this stage that the perpetrators have gambled on these precise acts of generosity.

Meanwhile, the police are investigating in all directions, but among other things, Shannon's family environment is also being targeted. After all, family members are often involved in cases of child abduction. Especially Michael Donovan, Craig's uncle, who is increasingly under surveillance - as is the mother herself. In the interviews, they repeatedly surprise the investigators with new explanations and become increasingly entangled in contradictions. In the end, six different versions are told. And the mother's behaviour is also increasingly erratic. A liaison officer of the police is very surprised at how the woman, who is so worried and in tears in the media, acts in her own four walls when it comes to the disappearance of her daughter. She barely looks up when the policewoman comes into the house but prefers to continue playing with her partner on the Xbox. And when the policewoman's phone rings - the ringing tone is a popular pop song - Karen suddenly gets up and starts dancing to the sound. At times, despair and worry are completely blown away.

On the 24th day, things finally start to move. At half past twelve on March 14 2008, the police gain access to a house in nearby Lidgate Gardens, Batley Carr. The home of 39-year-old, Michael Donovan. He is the uncle of Karen's partner, Craig Meehan. The police search the filthy apartment building and have the right nose: Under a bed they make a shocking discovery. Here lies nine-year-old Shannon Matthews. drugged and tied up so she can't run away. Someone has tied her to a beam with an elastic rope. The girl is struggling to articulate herself and keeps passing out. Donovan, who is in the house, is arrested on the spot. For the policemen it is clear: Either he is the sole kidnapper, or he is at least significantly involved in the kidnapping.

However, something else disturbing is discovered: the laptop of Karen's partner Craig Meehan. And 136 child pornography images are stored on it. Investigators are appalled.

The police immediately suspect that others may be involved in the "kidnapping". So, they take the little girl into custody and hand her over to the local youth welfare office. In Britain, section 46 of the Children Act 1989 allows the police to hold children in custody for up to 72 hours for their protection. But even on March 17, Shannon does not return to her mother. When the little girl is asked if she would like to, she denies it vehemently and explains to the police officers that she would rather just be with her favourite cat. Instead, the severely traumatised Shannon is put into a foster family. She suffers from violent nightmares and needs intensive psychiatric care. The police questioning of the child takes several weeks.

What the public has not yet suspected: the noose around Karen Matthews is tightening more and more. Incriminating evidence is emerging that suggests that the mother is not as uninvolved in the bizarre abduction as she would like to make out. Craig Meehan's mother, for example, records a strange phone conversation in which a voice is heard in the background that sounds strongly like Shannon's. Karen tells the person in the background to keep quiet. And finally, Karen herself confesses to her friends that she has been involved in the crime. On a car ride with acquaintances, she blabs out. Shocked, the acquaintances confront Karen with their suspicions, whereupon she explains that she and Donovan have conspired. His job was to take care of her daughter - but unfortunately, everything went wrong. What Karen does not suspect is that the police are already so suspicious of the victim's family that this car is being bugged. The recorded confession is the last missing piece of the puzzle in the investigation. Karen Matthews will be arrested immediately.

When the hoax comes out, the public's mood changes, the fellow citizens are extremely upset and feel cheated. Instead of sympathy and understanding, hate now fills the headlines. A real public shitstorm breaks out over Karen Matthews. Among other things, she is called "the mother of all lies". How can a mother do such a horrible thing to her daughter? The opinion of the chief investigator of the West Yorkshire police force Andy B. is clear: "Karen Matthews is pure evil" and in the newspapers Karen is titled "Britain's worst mother". Even years later, in 2020, the British press still keeps a close eye on this woman, informs the public of her every step, of course, with devotion, about every misstep.

During the court case, the terrible truth about the conspiracy comes to light. It is revealed that such feelings as motherly love and parental guidance are obviously foreign to Karen Matthew. In fact, it appears that Donovan and Matthews merely staged the entire kidnapping story in order to collect a large reward and make themselves rich. The fact that they ended up waving in excess of £50,000 was a particularly pleasant side effect, but it was only as a result of public interest and sympathy.

The two planned to release Karen's daughter unharmed in the end. Donovan would then pretend to have discovered her by chance and go to a police station with the girl. The reward he was then entitled to was to be split between him and Karen.

Whoever would have thought that the two accomplices would protect each other and would rather remain silent than betray the other would be severely disappointed. There is no such thing as "honour among thieves" here. So, Donovan tries to exonerate himself by going on record that he was only supposed to take care of Shannon for a few days. Karen had even threatened him with violence if he didn't play along. She, on the other hand, said in tears on November 27 that she had nothing whatsoever to do with the kidnapping. Instead, her partner Craig Meehan ordered her to take the blame under threat of violence. On cross-examination, the prosecutor therefore tells her that she is telling "one lie after another".

But that's not all: Karen even tries to drag her mother into the whole thing. Allegedly, she knew where Shannon was all along; a conversation with her father is supposed to serve as proof. June Matthews, Karen's mother, can refute this accusation, however, because until his funeral, Karen demonstrably had no contact with her father.

It is also shocking what the forensic toxicologist who examined Shannon's hair has to report. It turns out that she was not only drugged during the 24 days, but that she had already been regularly administered a benzodiazepine, or temazepam to be precise - and probably had been for up to 20 months! This has a strong sedative effect and is therefore used as a sleeping pill. However, these drugs become addictive after a short time.

With regard to Craig Meehan, it turns out that he is not involved in the kidnapping conspiracy. Because of the child pornographic content on his computer he receives a prison sentence of 20 weeks. However, numerous questions arise regarding his person: What kind of relationship did the 22-year-old, and the older Karen Matthews have if he was not privy to the whole thing? Shouldn't he have noticed something, for example her sometimes rather emotionally uninvolved behaviour? And is there possibly a connection with his obviously existing paedophile preferences? Meehan's exact role will raise many questions in public discourse in the period to come.

Finally, on December 4, sentences will be handed down at Leeds Crown Court: Donovan is guilty of kidnapping and false imprisonment. Matthews is guilty of child abuse and obstruction of justice. Both are each sentenced to eight years imprisonment.

The judge described this act as "truly abominable" in the sentencing. In addition, Karen is deprived of custody of all seven children, who are placed in different foster families. For their protection, Shannon and the others are also given a new identity.

Karen is lucky in the end: after just four years she is released from prison in 2012. She also receives a new identity for protection and moves to the southwest of England, where she wants to build a new life for herself. Not only has she changed her appearance, but she has become a born-again Christian and works in the social sector. She also hopes to get in touch with her children again. However, it turns out that even now Karen is still hard on the edge of legality. She loses her job after becoming "too close" to the husband of a pensioner whose wife she was caring for. On another occasion, she was discovered selling donated food to homeless people.

An old friend of Matthews, Julie Bushby, has recently spoken out. She is convinced that Karen at least cannot have been the main culprit in the kidnapping conspiracy and even publicly demands a retrial. Bushby sees Matthews more as a kind of victim and suspects that she wanted to separate from Craig Meehan and move out of the shared apartment. That's why she had let Shannon move in with Meehan's uncle in advance, but due to pressure from friends and family, she backed off from the separation at the last moment and thought up the kidnapping as an attempt to explain her daughter's disappearance. Bushby, however, also believes that Matthews could not have conceived of such a complex deception. Truth or the attempt to see something good in an old friend?

At Christmas 2019, Karen Matthews gets engaged to a craftsman. Months earlier, she had told journalists, "I'm not the worst mother in Britain." Her reasoning is astounding: "I didn't kill anyone." She actually believes this, because on her bedside table there is a decorative object, of the type sold in gift shops, souvenir shops and also in supermarkets. It bears squiggly, sentimental lettering decorated with bright colours, and it stands next to a photo of Matthew's children, who have long since wanted nothing more to do with her. The ornament reads: Best Mum…

CHAPTER SIX:

"Britain's most wanted man"
(by Puppies and Crime)

"On October 11, 2015, my life changed forever," says Tracey Hanson in an interview. She has tears in her eyes, and her voice trembles.

"He was taken from us in the most horrible way - suddenly, abruptly, viciously and violently. I have no words to express the pain that consumes me every day, but we will forever be grateful to everyone who helped bring Josh's killer to justice after four long, painful years.

"This has been an incredibly difficult journey and along with the police, we would like to extend our special thanks to friends, family, and the public, who have helped us through our darkest hours with news of support and help in sharing Josh's story.

"While we have received justice, I have been sentenced to a life term without our wonderful Josh."

It all begins 21 years before the act that made Tracy Hanson's life so completely unhinged in 2015.

Josh Hanson is born February 27, 1994 at Central Middlesex Hospital. He is a bright child, curious about the world and life. He has a gentle, friendly character and an infectious laugh to match. His elder sister Brooke is four years older; they go through thick and thin together, taking care of, and standing up for each other. There is a deep sibling love between them that continues. Even as adults, the two remain inseparable, going on holiday with friends, dancing, and drinking.

Josh is enrolled at West Herts College in Watford, where he is studying sports science. His goal is to be a successful personal trainer one day.

During the summer semester holidays, Josh wants to use his free time to earn money and gain work experience. He is applying for a position in the administration of Standmore Quality Surfacing Ltd, a road construction company and will be hired directly. The company is excited about Josh, happy to have a pleasant new team member.

"Britain's most wanted man"

It's October 11, 2015, an ordinary English autumn day. It is cloudy and cool with a light wind and Josh accompanies his girlfriend to the hospital. There they visit her sick father. After saying goodbye and leaving the hospital, they want to end the evening relaxed in the company of friends and family. They go to the RE Bar in Hillingdon, a district in the north of London. The evening is cheerful, the atmosphere is relaxed, and the bar is completely full. People laugh, drink and party like every weekend.

But the cheerful, carefree hustle and bustle will soon come to an abrupt end.

"Last order", they say at 1 am and the barman rings in the last round.

A man in his early 30s gets up and leaves the table where he and his friends were sitting. He walks straight up to Josh, who is standing at the bar to order a last round of drinks for himself and his friends.

"What is your problem?" the man suddenly asks Josh. The tone is aggressive and challenging. Josh doesn't feel addressed by the stranger, though. He doesn't know him and has never seen him before. Suddenly, the man pulls out a knife.

The movement is lightning fast. Everything takes only fractions of a second. The stranger stabs Josh. The cut goes from the ear, over the neck, and to the chest. 37 centimetres long.

Everything happens much too fast. So fast that the people present do not even realise what has just happened. Then, they are paralyzed from shock. The bleeding cannot be stopped. Josh collapses and bleeds to death on the spot, in the full bar, between friends and strangers.

"We were 10 minutes away, we never got the chance to say goodbye", Tracey, the mother describes her pain and grief. "I was denied my place as Josh's mother. He lay alone on the cold floor, I couldn't hold him in my arms to comfort or reassure him, to give him hope that everything would be OK."

The strange attacker quietly, calmly, and secretly, leaves the bar after his deed. His name is Shane O'Brien. Shane was born in Ladbroke Grove. He's 6'1", with grey eyes and brown hair. He's a father of two and a big boxing and martial arts fan.

His escape and the search for him will keep the whole of England on tenterhooks for years to come. Soon the press will award him the significant title "Britain's Most Wanted Man".

After his brutal deed, he first hides in a trailer park in Camber Sands, East Sussex. When the police launch a Facebook appeal, asking the local population for help,

"Britain's most wanted man"

O'Brien is identified by the staff of the local pub. His fingerprints were also previously found there on a glass. Before the police can arrest him, he manages to fly from England to the Netherlands in a private plane with the help of "Vanessa", who is hiding behind the name. "Vanessa" will never be found. What is certain is that he or she won't be the only helping hand Shane has in his ongoing escape from justice.

Although he is now out of the country, the police continue their search.

MURDER. 50,000 GBP REWARD. (approx. 59 000 Euro) The police posters seem to be omnipresent and occupy public space. Interpol and Europol are also involved in the manhunt. The transnational organisations include O'Brien on their "most wanted" lists.

But Shane is clever and shrewd, he knows how to fly under the radar and evade police intervention. A real cat-and-mouse game begins. A terrible, gruelling time for Josh's family, who fervently hope and pray that the murderer of their son and brother will be held accountable for this horrible act.

But the perpetrator pulls out all the stops: To escape arrest, Shane O'Brien lets his hair and beard grow. He has the date of birth of his child, which adorns his body as a tattoo, cut out. He even obtains forged identity papers.

For a long time, the escape goes well. With the help of friends, he succeeds in living underground. He travels to Dubai, Germany, the Czech Republic, and Belgium. Changes his whereabouts again and again. Before the authorities can track him down, the young man moves on again.

In 2017, O'Brien is arrested for assault under the alias "Enzo Melloncelli". But once again chance comes to his rescue: he is released on bail before the police officers realise that this Enzo Melloncelli is in fact Shane O'Brien, an internationally wanted murderer.

For Shane, it is a warning shot. A sign that it is time to decamp and move on. So, Shane is long gone by the time the authorities realise their mistake.

Despite this failure, the feverish search continues.

On March 23, 2019, the redeeming news finally arrives! Shane O'Brien is arrested in Romania and transferred to Great Britain on April 5, 2019. Here he will finally be put on trial.

Yet everyone - Josh's family, the judges, the world - is really only concerned with one question: Why? Why did Shane O'Brien kill Josh? What drives a person to suddenly attack a complete stranger with a knife, to slit him open and end his life?

When Shane is confronted with this question during the trial, his answer sounds as banal as it is absurd. His simple reasoning: Josh's body language had an aggressive effect on him.

"I felt threatened when I approached him and thought it was possible that he might be armed."

"Did you see a gun?" The prosecutor asks. The answer is - no.

It is a rejoinder that raises many questions: Why did O'Brien think Josh was threatening? Why wasn't he able to just walk away? To avoid the perceived threat? Why was he even carrying a knife? What goes on in a man who decides to take a human life in a matter of seconds?

The videos from the surveillance camera are also being evaluated, everyone is hoping for further insights - but no results. No special features can be detected on the recordings. Business as usual. The jury and the prosecutor cannot detect any behaviour that could have possibly provoked Shane's crime.

O'Brien's version of the events of the evening is, of course, quite different. He felt that Josh's group was not happy that he was sitting at a table near them that night. Hostility would have been in the air.

"This bar is very small. Body language alone can create an atmosphere," explains the perpetrator in search of reasons for his actions.

"It certainly can if you're looking for it, Mr. O'Brien," replies the prosecutor.

So, is the confinement in a room filled with celebrating people supposed to have been the reason for the cold-blooded murder?

Shane adds: "I assure you from the bottom of my heart, I did not mean to touch him with that blade." He tells the court he was just trying to scare Josh. Just "pretend" that he was going to hurt him.

The jury doesn't believe this story, they think O'Brien's explanations are simply subterfuge. 55 minutes of deliberation is all the jury needs to reach a verdict: Guilty as charged. The verdict: Shane O'Brien will spend at least 26 years in prison for the murder of Josh Hanson.

The trial ends with the following words from the judge:

"This was a grotesque, violent, and totally unnecessary attack on an innocent man. The reason why you behaved in this way can never be fully explained. However, you know the reason."

Even if Shane knows why he was so brutal that night, it doesn't matter to the relatives of his victim. How much more does it benefit Josh's mother Tracey and his girlfriend to know why they lost their beloved Josh? No explanation can ever bring him back. His girlfriend will probably never be able to erase this traumatic event and the images of the evening from her memory. What remains is the painful memory of Josh and his life, which has come to a far too early end.

Between all the grief and trauma, Josh's family still manage to find some strength to create something to preserve his memory.

His mother Tracey sets up the Josh Hanson Trust, a foundation whose goal is to fight and investigate knife attacks and assaults. They want to show alternatives and encourage people to rethink. The declared aim is to avoid fates like Josh's, so that no more sons and daughters are senselessly torn from life. The mother describes this project as a "legacy of the positive, love and compassion in Josh's name," as she puts it.

She is sure that this is how Josh would have wanted it.

CHAPTER SEVEN:

A majestic nightgown

When the details of this case were first released in the summer of 1982, it almost meant the end of the political career of the British Home Secretary, Willie Whitelaw. First, Viscount Whitelaw was an important advisor to Prime Minister Margaret Thatcher, who assisted the "Iron Lady", especially in the Falklands crisis from April to June 1982. The conservative politician of Scottish descent feels forced to offer his resignation virtually overnight. For he is unable to explain the disastrous security loopholes and mistakes that were revealed in the night of July 9 and also four weeks earlier. And this happens in Buckingham Palace of all places. The debacle, which even threatens the careers of other important politicians and causes a worldwide sensation, is triggered by an Irishman with a mischievous smile, who now knows what the Queen wears in bed at night.

Michael Fagan, a Briton of Irish descent, was born in 1950 in Clerkenwell, London, as the first of three children of Michael and Ivy Fagan. His father is a steelworker and also a master locksmith. However, Michael junior does not last long at home as there are problems, owing to his father's tendency to drink and get violent. Therefore, at the age of 16, Michael moves out and finds work as a painter and decorator, but he will never really feel at home in the "normal working world". Instead, Fagan junior oscillates between petty crime, drugs, and recurring difficulties, into which he manoeuvres himself with masterful skill. His father will later describe him as a very content, happy person, who always has a good connection to other people and can chat with them with ease. In fact, Michael Fagan has an extremely relaxed charisma. Around the eyes of the dark-haired, slim man with full lips, are numerous laughter lines, which are a visible sign that we are dealing with a man full of unusual ideas and humour.

In 1982, Fagan is 32 years old, once again unemployed, and his relationship with his wife Christine, with whom he has been married for 10 years and has four children with, is in crisis. When Christine leaves him on June 7, this is a real drama for the fun-loving man, which throws him

A majestic nightgown

completely off course. Although Fagan has spent a merry evening in the pub, he still feels completely confused. There are at least two different versions of what follows: The more amusing reports state that on July 9, drunk Fagan made a crazy bet with some guests at the pub for 5 pounds each. He wants to make it to see the Queen. With the collected bets in his pocket, the unemployed painter and decorator calls a taxi to take him to Buckingham Palace. Fagan even explains to the driver what he is up to - but he only laughs at the drunkard's supposed joke. For the young man wants to convince the Queen to give him a kiss.

According to another version, the completely desperate Fagan wanders aimlessly through the streets of the British capital until he suddenly realises that he has landed himself in front of Buckingham Palace. And at that moment, a completely crazy thought is said to have crossed his mind.

Fagan climbs over the gate, which is located near the Ambassador's Residence. He stays for a while in the room where the royal stamp collection is located, which was created by King George V and is said to be worth several million pounds. What the intruder doesn't know is that he accidentally sets off an alarm here twice - but incredibly, it is simply ignored and turned off by the police, who assume it is a false alarm

Finally, Fagan continues his expedition through the palace. The nine-metre high, barbed-wire reinforced walls can't scare him off. He climbs over one and then continues up a rain gutter - up to the roof. Here, too, he triggers an alarm, or would have done so if the alarms had been correctly activated. On the roof, the talented facade climber, who is unkempt and "slightly tipsy", takes off the sandals he is wearing and simply leaves them there. That way it's easier. The daredevil finds his way into the palace via a small projection on the façade, because a window is open in the wing of the royal family's apartments, of all places.

Once inside, the intruder begins to leisurely stroll around the corridors. Although it is already shortly before 7 o'clock in the morning, there is still a relative calmness, so that Fagan can let the impressions affect him. He is a little disappointed as the royal residence seems very ordinary to him and no money seems to have been wasted on decoration. Fagan's impression is that everything is "dusty", with "creaking floorboards".

On his walk, Fagan even encounters a maid who believes he is an employee - despite his unkempt appearance and missing shoes. Since she believes that security matters are not her responsibility, she does not stop the man. The problems with the alarm systems in the building also continue. Either the guards think the signals are a false alarm and turn them off, or the systems are not activated to begin with.

It is unclear whether Fagan actually knocked down a heavy crystal ashtray on his "private sightseeing tour" and injured his hand in the process, as is reported in some places. Allegedly, he is said to have carried the large shard further with him. He himself refrains from describing this detail.

When Fagan strolls past the Queen's private chambers and looks at paintings, the bodyguard's armchair in front of the door is empty. Paul Whybrew has left his guard position for a short time to walk the guard dogs of Queen Elizabeth II, a British dog breed called Corgis. Assumedly, the empty armchair is the sign for Fagan that an important person is sleeping here. And the drunken man thinks it is an excellent idea to see how a queen sleeps.

Carefully, he opens the door and enters the bedroom around 7 am. The man is surprised that the room is smaller than he imagined it to be. He describes the furnishings and decoration as "very simple". Quietly, he approaches the bed, around which curtains are drawn. Fagan pulls a curtain to the side and suddenly finds himself standing directly in front of the Queen of Great Britain, who is sleeping deep and solidly under her feather blanket in her double bed. Alone. Which surprises Fagan because he was also expecting her husband, Prince Philip, to be there.

Then Queen Elizabeth II suddenly wakes up!

Regarding what follows, there are again two versions. In the media, it is reported that Fagan sits at the foot of the bed and chats with the queen for about ten minutes. Allegedly, the conversation is an attempt to calm the intruder and lull him to safety until help arrives. Meanwhile, the Queen is said to have triggered the alarm under her bed at least twice - but without success, because the alarm button is not connected. When Fagan finally asks her for a cigarette, she calls a footman, who then alarms the police.

According to another version, Fagan is said to have threatened to slit his wrists with the crystal shard he brought with him. After the queen sets off the alarm, she and a maid lure Fagan to a nearby tea kitchen when he asks for a cigarette.

The version Fagan tells 30 years later is much less spectacular - but probably closer to reality. When the then 56-year-old Queen suddenly sits up, she just shouts: "Get out! Get out!" and jumps out of bed. The man is as shocked as the little woman in front of him and starts to tremble. "What are you actually doing here?" the queen

A majestic nightgown

demands in a cutting voice before she runs out of the room barefoot.

The burglar catches a glimpse of the Queen's knee-length nightgown, a model with a colourful, large Liberty Print - a detail that will cause quite a stir in the media afterwards.

Outside the door, Elizabeth II finally bumps into her bodyguard Paul Whybrew, who has returned from the alleyway. The unarmed footman will not let Fagan out of his sight until the police arrive. However, the intruder's distraught state does not escape him. So, he says to him: "Buddy, you look like you could use a drink" and takes Fagan to the Queen's tea kitchen. There he pours him a proper sip of whiskey of the brand "Famous Grouse" from the Queen's private stock. Together they wait for the police.

This almost unbelievable incident causes a lot of attention, especially because the investigation reveals that the adventurous Irishman Fagan had already been to Buckingham Palace four weeks earlier.

About a month earlier, on the night of June 7, shortly after his wife ended things, Fagan breaks into the Palace for the first time. While in July he only roams Buckingham Palace for about an hour, he spends almost the entire night in the building that evening and finally leaves it undetected. Fagan also tries to climb up the rain gutter on this occasion but is unsuccessful. Then he climbs through an open window into the bedroom of a chambermaid - who is present. The completely horrified woman immediately runs to the security service. But when they examine the room, Fagan has already left. He sneaks along the corridors undetected, rummaging here and there through the rooms. For example, he enters a room crammed with gifts for the new-born son of Prince Charles and Princess Diana, Prince William, who was born two weeks earlier. Lots of teddy bears and cups.

During this exploratory tour he cannot discover the Queen's chambers, instead Fagan passes rooms where there are signs with the names "Diana" and "Charles". He treats himself to some crackers with cheese that are standing around and plays "Goldilocks and the Three Bears" in a throne room. He tries out every throne chair and tries to find out which one the Queen is sitting on. In the process, the burglar admires the works of art on the walls.

However, Fagan is mainly looking for a toilet. Although all rooms have signs with names on them, he can't find the saving words "toilet" anywhere. He is reluctant to relieve himself on the expensive carpets. When he sees a few bowls with the inscription "Corgi Futter", this is his opportunity ...

A majestic nightgown

On this occasion, he enters the room of Prince Charles, who is not present. Here Fagan helps himself to a bottle of wine. A cheap drop from California, as he always adds later. He sits down at the desk and puts his feet on the tabletop. Since Fagan can't find a corkscrew, he presses the cork into the bottle and treats himself to half the contents. At this moment he suddenly asks himself: "Oh, my God, where am I right now?" and decides to leave as quickly as possible.

In fact, getting out of Buckingham Palace turns out to be considerably more difficult than getting in. Eventually, however, Fagan finds a door through which he enters the back garden. He only has to climb over a wall, then the intruder is again safe and sound on the famous red-bricked road, "The Mall".

A few days after this first palace expedition, Fagan is arrested for car theft and is held in custody for three weeks. He had stolen a car in London to follow his wife to Stonehenge. On July 8, the Irishman is released - and directly one day later, on Tuesday, he gets into Buckingham Palace for the second time.

Fagan still cannot explain his reason for doing this. He suspects that magic mushrooms might have been to blame. Because five months earlier he had put magic mushrooms in his soup - but not the small handful as recommended, but a good amount. Two years later, he would still have felt that he was just starting to get off the trip. Drugs are actually something that always play a big role in Fagan's life.

The extreme security deficiencies at Buckingham Palace, which were revealed by Fagan's action, create a scandal that causes worldwide excitement in the following days. Even Willie Whitelaw, the then British Home Secretary, is offering to resign as chief constable of the police. However, this is rejected by the Queen herself. After the incident, some security officers are replaced, alarm systems in Buckingham Palace are renewed, and security measures are made much stricter, and even tightly measured.

The incident is also a shock for Fagan's family; his father is so upset about it that he gets a stress-related heart attack. Something that his son deeply regrets. Previously, the father had described his son to the media as a "huge Royal fan" who had done all this just to show how easy it is to get into the palace.

Michael Fagan is accused, but the whole thing turns out very mildly for him. Due to the massive security deficiencies in the palace, he cannot be proven to have broken in or trespassed. The court gives him the benefit of the fact that the numerous defects or deactivation of the alarm systems and also mistakes made by the security staff

A majestic nightgown

made the incident possible and promoted it. Ultimately, he can only be accused of stealing a bottle of wine - and this offence is so minor that the Briton of Irish descent will not be convicted. What Fagan cannot avoid, however, is that he is committed to a psychiatric hospital for six months. Following his stay, he is released without any findings, so he is mentally healthy.

One year later, in 1983, Fagan's fame begins to fade again, so he produces a record together with the punk rock band "The Bollock Brothers", a cover of the famous song by the legendary Sex Pistols "God Save the Queen". Since this recording can be considered a curiosity at best, the success remains extremely modest - and Fagan returns to what he did before. Again and again he comes into conflict with the law - often because of trifles. In 1984 Fagan attacks a policeman in a café in Wales, and three years later he is convicted for indecent exposure. When he reunites with his ex-wife Christine, the couple begin dealing heroin together with one of their sons. But the police put a quick end to the family's activities and Fagan is then sent to prison for another 4 years.

36 years after the legendary incident in which Fagan got to see the Queen's nightgown, he believes that he actually did the Royal Family a real favour with his action. After all, this is how the serious safety deficiencies came to light;

without this, nobody would have noticed for a long time. At least, that's how Michael Fagan sees it, but whether the Windsor family felt the same way remains questionable.

By the way, they sent him his sandals in 1984, which he left on the roof during his "burglary". Very courteous!

CHAPTER EIGHT:

Cut up faces
(by Puppies and Crime)

Levi Bellfield is popular, funny, and courteous. A man who playfully wraps women around his finger and makes men think he's their best friend. His neighbours appreciate his helpfulness. He looks after the apartments of his acquaintances when they are away on holiday. He is the perfect friend and neighbour. And a ticking time bomb. Because if you look closer, the beautiful facade crumbles. A facade that he has carefully pulled up and behind which the other Levi hides.

The Levi who lurks behind the façade, plagued by humiliating childhood memories, who hates women, who is addicted to control, and who thinks everyone is his enemy. He can still hear the laughter of the other children in his head, taunting him because he is small and weak.

But there is more: there are also the unpleasant rumours going around about him. They call him "bugsy" because he is said to have consorted with his sister's rabbit. Even the giggles of the beautiful girls who want nothing to do with him still echo in his head.

Then, at home as a child, after running the gauntlet in the hostile world, Levi sinks into the arms of his mother and his only confidant. She treats him like the wounded child he sees himself as. Until his teenage years, she spoils the boy like a toddler. She cares for and caresses him. Levi and his mother have a particularly close relationship - in fact, they are already mutually dependent. A relationship that will shape him forever.

The insecurity and fear of childhood develops over time into anger and firm determination. Never again will anyone laugh at him. He wants to be strong and manly. Levi also does not shy away from pumping up his muscles with steroids to achieve this goal. As a bouncer in a nightclub, he now decides who is allowed to join in and who has to shiver outside in the cold.

However, the sneering laughter of the beautiful girls from his childhood forever torments him. Perhaps to compensate for these experiences, Levi seeks partners whom he can control and dominate. They have to cut up his food and even taste it.

Cut up faces

While the anger, hatred and insecurity continue to ferment in Levi, his friendly facade works. It holds and earns him prestige and the trust of his fellow men. But the clock in the man ticks on inexorably and counts down to zero. Every day he is one step closer to the inevitable explosion.

It is the beginning of 2002. 13-year-old Amanda Jane Dowler, known as Milly, lives with her family in Walton-on-Thames, a small town about a half hour drive from London.

On March 21, 2002 Milly leaves Heathside School in Weybridge at 3:07 pm and goes with a friend to Weybridge Station where they board the train together. The girls get off at Walton-on-Thames Station, one stop before their usual stop in Hersham, and go to the station café for dinner. After Milly calls her father at 3:47 p.m. to inform him that she will be home in half an hour. The girls leave the café at 4:05 p.m. and each make their way home alone. A few minutes later, Milly is seen by a friend of her sister walking along the street, laughing and waving. This is the last time anyone sees the girl alive.

At 7:00 p.m., Milly is finally reported missing by her parents. A nationwide search for her begins. Hundreds of police comb the forests, rivers, and roads surrounding Hersham. Even helicopters are used to search for the missing girl.

A week later, despite an intensive search, there is still no trace of Milly. The police are at a loss and assume that Milly was not kidnapped but ran away on her own accord. After all, there are no indications of a crime having been committed.

But how likely is it that a 13-year-old girl would simply run away? All alone? For that long? Wouldn't she at least leave a note or pack a bag with essentials?

As much as Milly's parents hope that their daughter has run away voluntarily, maybe gone on an adventure, is doing well somewhere, they can't get anything out of the police theory. Because this is not the Milly they know and love. And they will be right. Their Milly will never come back and knock on their door again.

After almost six uncertain months between hope and desperation, mushroom pickers discover human remains in the Yateley Heath Woods near Yateley, Hampshire, on September 18, 2002. The dental findings bring the sad certainty - it is Milly. Due to the advanced decomposition of the body, the cause of death cannot be determined. What is astonishing is that the body has been completely stripped. No clothing or possessions will ever be found.

The missing persons case now becomes a murder investigation. A murder investigation that will take many years. In which traces will keep popping up that lead nowhere. Horrible phone calls and e-mails to the parents that their daughter has been caught by a human trafficking ring. All lies, as it turns out years later. Lies which, by then, have nearly driven the family mad.

Marsha McDonnell is a talented musician and is described by people as "calm and hardworking". Before starting her studies, the young woman wants to discover the wide world and plans to travel to the other end of the earth to Australia. However, she will never make this journey.

In February 2003, Marsha is on her way home from a movie night with her friends. She is only a few meters away from her house in Hampton, southwest London, when she is brutally attacked. Someone hits the 18-year-old from behind on the head with a blunt object, several times, and the young woman goes straight to the ground. The perpetrator simply leaves the badly injured Marsha lying there. Two days later, the future musician dies in hospital from her injuries.

The police are left with a mystery. There are no witnesses to the crime, no helpful evidence to suggest the murderer or his motive. Only the murder weapon is the subject of some speculation. Based on the autopsy findings, it is assumed that the blunt object could have been a hammer.

Statistically speaking, most victims know their killers. Usually, they are friends, acquaintances, or family members. Only in very few cases do the perpetrators not know their victims. But in Marsha's case, the investigators quickly exclude all acquaintances of having any involvement. No one has a motive, there's no evidence to support it. Is there a mad killer on the streets of London? One who randomly selects his victims entirely at will? One who doesn't follow a pattern?

On May 28, 2004, more than a year after the attack on Marsha, 18-year-old Kate Sheedy is hit by a white van while crossing a street in an industrial estate in Isleworth. Luckily, she survives. After several weeks in hospital she can resume her normal life. The case is reported and published.

At first glance, this case has little to do with the deadly attack on Marsha. But if you look closer, only the murder weapon is different. If you replace the hammer with the car, there are parallels, which unfortunately are recognised much too late.

Amélie Delagrange is a 22-year-old French exchange student. After missing the bus, she decides to make her way on foot in the mild summer night of August 19, 2004. However, this proves to be a fatal decision as she runs straight into the hands of her murderer. Amélie is found seriously injured in Twickenham Green and that very night she dies in hospital from severe head injuries.

Cut up faces

What is at first only a suspicion, now slowly becomes certainty: a serial killer is on the move in London. A murderer who seems to have no real motive and kills out of pure murderous lust. There is no connection between Marsha, Amélie and later Kate. The young women didn't know each other, had no mutual friends. Yet they fell victim to the same hand. The lack of connection presents the investigators with an almost impossible task. Or is it significant that they all have blond hair?

The case of Amélie Delagrange is assigned to Detective Chief Inspector Colin Sutton, although he is relatively inexperienced in murder investigations and there is hardly any useful evidence for him to work with.

The police are now looking for a killer who targets young blonde women. He is apparently not interested in sex, but in hurting and killing. But why did he want to extinguish the lives of these young women? He is compared to a hunter on the prowl, who watches his victims and feels superior to his "prey". The mysterious perpetrator leaves no evidence behind. Hardly any mistakes are made, and he plans his attacks carefully. There are no DNA traces, but in the case of Amélie something has disappeared. Amélie's mobile phone. Could this be a valuable lead? Could the killer have taken the phone as a trophy? Sutton and his team managed to get the phone company's data on the device. And this evaluation contains an important hint: A few minutes after the attack, the device loses the network for a moment. At that time, the phone was located in Walton-on-Thames, far away from the crime scene. So, the murderer is mobile. He is probably travelling by car.

On video surveillance near the crime scene, a suspicious white van stands out. One of 24,000 white vans registered in the UK. It's a small, seemingly unimportant lead. A marginal note. But Sutton's following up on it. In a single clue file on the case of Kate Sheedy and a white van, the investigator then finds the testimony of a certain Jo Collins. She claims that her ex-partner owns a white van and hates blond women. She said that he was a violent man and that she thought he might kill her. She also reported that, in his house, she found a magazine in which blond women's faces were cut up. This makes the investigators sit up and take notice. The ex-partner of whom Jo Collins reports is called Levi Bellfield and is now the main suspect in the Amélie Delagrange case.

Born on May 17, 1968 in Isleworth, London, Levi Bellfield is one of five children in a Roma family. When the little boy is 10 years old, his father dies of leukaemia. A heavy blow of fate that brings Levi and his mother closer together. She cares for him and pampers him. Maybe because of the loss of his father, she always lets Levi know how special he is.

Levi remains dependent on his mother's affection until adulthood. He is unable to emotionally emancipate himself from her and thus to develop freely and normally. At the age of 13, he is already caught in petty theft. But nothing happens. He experiences no consequences for the offences, which results in a feeling of superiority over the police.

At the age of 21, he meets his first wife, with whom he will have 5 children.

Outwardly not an attractive man, Levi knows how to win women over with his eloquence and his nonchalant manner. He sees himself as a gift to the female sex, which has to obey him unconditionally as a reward for his attention. One says in retrospect that the women were only allowed to speak when he allowed it. Only cook what he likes. Only go to the toilet when he accompanied them. They were allowed to have a mobile phone, on which the only number stored was Levi's.

He, however, has many partners. Likes to be in and out of relationships.

Every day he hits his partners - but not in the face. He is too smart for that. That would leave visible marks. But none of the women dares to report him. Again, he gets away with his behaviour. In the meantime, he feels untouchable. Superior.

But when the police come with a search warrant, he hides naked in the attic. The police discover him and take him away.

During the interrogation, Bellfield refuses to testify, turns his back demonstratively to the police, and stares stubbornly at the wall. His behaviour resembles that of a defiant child.

After 18 months in custody, Levi Bellfield is charged on March 2, 2006 with the murder of Amélie and the attempted murder of Kate. The murder of Marsha is added as a further charge on May 25, 2006. The trial begins on October 12, 2007 and Levi Bellfield pleads not guilty to all charges.

He follows the trial emotionlessly, seeming downright bored. Only when he testifies does Levi take action trying to wrap the jury around his finger with his notorious charm. Without success. The circumstantial evidence weighs heavily. There are several video recordings that show him driving aimlessly around in his white van. Like a hunter in search of his prey.

On February 25 2008, Levi is found guilty and sentenced to life imprisonment. One day after the verdict of guilty, another charge is brought against him. This time it is about the murder of Milly. There is a lot of evidence pointing to Bellfield: his place of residence, video recordings showing how the red car of his girlfriend at the time, which he had borrowed, circles around the crime scene and a colleague of Levi testifies that he confessed the murder of Milly to her in 2002. She thought it was nonsense, pomposity, a lie.

Bellfield obviously enjoys this trial; he instructs his lawyer to tear Milly's family apart in court. He is enjoying one last time in public, living out his destructive side. Again, he is found guilty and receives a second life sentence - without the possibility of probation.

In 2016, still in prison, Levi describes the murder of Milly in all the gruesome and horrible details. A confession! But he withdraws this right afterwards. Is it a cry for attention, or does he just want to play a sadistic game with the relatives of his victims? For Milly's family, it feels as if he has killed Milly a second time.

For Levi's ex-partner, Jo, he is pure evil. He is unscrupulous, cold, and only concerned with his own advantage. Many people will agree with her because the facts speak for themselves. Is it a hidden clue or rather irony of fate that this man is called Levi? Because if you rearrange the letters, they spell the word – Evil.

CHAPTER NINE:

The fallen angel

Normally, it is a real no-go among colleagues to search each through other's computer, possibly even their e-mails. Because even if you are only supposed to use your work computer for work, it still probably holds something private. In this respect, it is not an easy decision for the colleague of IT consultant Colin Blanchard from Rochdale, Greater Manchester, to sit at his computer on June 5, 2009. But the 49-year-old Colin is on a business trip in Dubai and everything points towards him stealing from the company.

The colleague takes one more deep breath, then boots the computer. Focused, he searches through the folders and files - there must be proof somewhere here! Sorting is meticulous, as usual with IT specialists, for whom logic and structure are essential. Nevertheless, the necessary information cannot be found. The colleague decides to venture into subfolders and also takes the precaution of looking into the more private folders.

When the first image file slowly opens, the colleague is surprised. Weren't Colin's children already much older? And what amateur cuts photographer off the heads of everyone in their pictures? But as his gaze wanders deeper, his fingers suddenly start to tremble. The mouse slips from his grip. A choking sound rises in his throat. He is overcome by such strong nausea that he hardly manages to close the disturbing picture that will haunt him forever. Only now, when he finally consciously looks at the small, infinite number of thumbnails in the folder, does he realise that the opened photo is not an isolated case.

Tears of rage and desperation stand in his eyes as he dials the number of the Greater Manchester Police. Something urgently needs to be done here to save these victims.

The police agree. Immediately after the haunting, highly emotional description from the caller, investigators make their way to the office of the IT consulting firm. The men know that speed is of the essence here, because if anyone involved gets wind of the discovery, evidence will disappear immediately. Among other potentially suspicious things, Colin Blanchard's business computers are therefore confiscated and taken to the police station.

Experts will take action immediately and quickly find what they are looking for. Obviously, the owner felt very safe and saw no need to hide things. In addition to numerous incriminating photographs, texts and e-mails are also tracked down, which give a rudimentary idea of the full extent of this terrible crime. It is a crime that has the whole of Britain startled, because it shows how easy it is to harm the most innocent of all.

The stocky Vanessa Sylvia George, née Marks, is a cheerful woman who is extremely popular with family, friends, and colleagues. Everyone loves the optimistic charisma of the married mother of two. And the same goes for the parents of the babies and toddlers, who the conscientious woman looks after daily as a nursery educator. You can see that she enjoys taking care of the little ones. In the private nursery "Little Ted's Day Care Centre", which is located on the premises of the Laira Green Primary School in Plymouth, it was considered a stroke of luck when the experienced woman with the pleasant charisma started working here in 2006. Two years later, in 2008, she is even called the soul of the whole. Lovingly and jokingly, her parents like to call her an "angel".

Vanessa George, who previously worked for six years as a school assistant and babysitter, is considered exemplary.

Not only has she never had any problems with the police, but everyone trusts her, and she is also considered a good mother and loving wife, who has been with her partner for twenty years.

But maybe that is exactly what makes Vanessa secretly restless. For the fun-loving woman with the figure of Rubens seems to be missing something. Maybe this is exactly the reason why the internet has such a fascination for her and will play an increasingly important role for her. In the beginning, she probably feels like most adults who move around on the net: she looks for old friends and acquaintances to reconnect with. But the year 2008 is above all the beginning of the golden age of forums for everything and everyone. In addition, chat rooms are coming up where you can write privately. Vanessa is now using the internet to make new contacts. And she discovers that anonymity makes it possible to express even the most intimate fantasies and find people who even share them. Obviously, an exciting experience for the married woman, whose sex life is certainly running in rather well-trodden tracks. Increasingly, you can find them in sex chats.

When Facebook comes up, Vanessa also logs on to this trendy platform and is active here. As someone who loves children and works as a nursery teacher, it is probably only natural for her to sign and support the campaign "Against Child Abuse".

The fallen angel

All this is not yet unusual. The fatal dynamic only arises when Vanessa George gets in touch with Colin Blanchard on Facebook. It is unclear when exactly this will happen, probably towards the end 2008, and it is also unclear whether the two of them even know their real names. But this meeting will be the trigger for unspeakable suffering.

Married for about 16 years, Colin Blanchard is a man who values a certain level in his life. As an IT consultant, he affords himself a large, detached house, overlooking the hills of Littleborough near Rochdale. He likes to treat himself: Besides a huge flat screen TV, he owns just about every hip computer game to exist. There are palm trees in the garden, which he had to have delivered with a crane. Now and then, Blanchard even likes to claim that he is a film producer, or that he flies around as a football star in his private jet. But nobody suspects Blanchard hides deeper abysses. The 8,000 pounds he owes to the electricity provider is still the least of his problems. He has a weakness for child pornography. In 2002, he was put on record for downloading images from the Internet; in 2007, however, his criminal record is deleted by default.

Maybe it's these dark fantasies that Vanessa and Colin exchange at some point. Their deepest sexual abysses, of which both are probably about the abuse of children. It is then only a few steps from pronouncement to the deed, especially since Vanessa George, as an educator, deals with the objects of her desire on a daily basis. Perhaps it is simply a kind of game between the two, a form of test of courage. Or does Vanessa want to bind the man more closely to her, who at some point even confesses his love to her?

Whatever the triggering thoughts are, in December 2008, the first attacks occur at the private nursery in Plymouth, which has places for around 60 children. The nursery schoolteacher starts taking photos of the children under her care. Apparently, a favourable opportunity presents itself, especially when she changes their diapers. No one registers, as she always finds opportunities to be alone with one of the children. She takes pictures of children between the ages of two and five, preferring those who cannot yet speak. Is this possibly a perfidious precaution? Likewise, the heads are always not visible in the pictures. An accident, perhaps? This is a common procedure in child pornography to prevent the victims from being identified.

But it does not stop there. The mother of two starts taking more sexually explicit pictures. More and more often she uses objects to introduce them - toothbrushes or even plastic miniature golf clubs. At least once she brings a sex toy from home to work. It is this increase that later leads the investigators to the conclusion that at some point, a competition of some sort must have developed to take the most perverse photo.

In total, the educator filmed and photographed 124 abusive actions against the children. For these "fun photos", as she calls them, she has her own second mobile phone. The pictures and films are then sent to the IT specialist from Rochdale. But George doesn't stop at sending Blanchard intimate photos of her own 14-year-old daughter. It almost goes without saying that the two also exchange pictures of themselves and address their most abysmal sexual desires. In the period from December 2008 to June 2009, there are around 10,000 contacts via telephone, SMS, e-mail, and messenger.

The whole affair takes on even wider implications when Angela Allen, a single mother from Bulwell, Nottingham, becomes involved in the abuse. Blanchard also met her on Facebook in September 2008, and he confessed his love to her. All three are of a similar age and have a similar interest: child abuse. But with Angela, who used to work as a prostitute and does not live in such an orderly situation as George and Blanchard, a new element seems to be added to the perverse "game". Maybe the contest is her idea, because Allen is later described by an investigator as "scary and evil". Her fantasies go even further; she dreams of rape and sodomy. And even a child abduction is discussed by the three.

Since George has the easiest access to potential victims, she is usually the initiator of abuse recordings. She then shares them with the others. At first only with Blanchard, but after he introduced her to "AngBank" aka Angela Allen, she sends the recordings directly to the woman in Bulwell, too. But the other two do not behave passively at all; they also send documents showing sexual acts with children. Many, especially the parents of the abused children, want to see Blanchard as the head of the child porn gang, but this is rather unlikely, as the direct wire of the two women proves. Rather, the man is probably a kind of "midwife" who helped release the slumbering evil longings and energies.

The particularly frightening thing about this trio of like-minded people is that they seem to feel completely safe while mercilessly using children to live out and stimulate their own sexual desires and lust. They apparently do not think for a moment about the consequences for the victims. Furthermore, all three of them seem to have no fear of being exposed and there are no effective security measures in place at the nursery to protect the victims from possible assaults. It has been proven that the three perpetrators communicate quite openly with each other, without encryption and the use of code words or similar.

In fact, reality even proves them right, because it is only by chance that the whole house of cards finally collapses. If Blanchard's colleague had not searched his computer, the activities of this circle of abusive paedophiles would probably have continued for a long time - and possibly even with a spiral of increasing brutality.

For the specialists of the Greater Manchester Police, after a brief review of the photos and films on Colin Blanchard's computer, it is clear that they must act immediately. The pictures are shocking, so heart-breaking, that even the most hardened investigators admit that they felt sick at the sight of them. For it is shown in detail how sexual acts are performed on infants and small children. But it is not yet clear who is involved in the acts. It is therefore even more important not to startle any of those involved prematurely, so that no one destroys evidence or possibly disappears. The paedophile perpetrators should be brought to justice and removed from circulation! That is the declared aim of the investigators.

The first arrest will take place on June 6 2009. When Colin Blanchard steps off the plane at Manchester Airport, on which he returned to England from Dubai, he is already expected. But it is not his wife who is standing in front of him when he wants to leave the gate. The policemen ask him politely, but with a stern face, to follow them. At the police station he is confronted with the accusations, then his laptop and smartphone are taken away from him to check them for incriminating material as well. And indeed: more of the child pornographic depictions can be found here. In the course of the in-depth investigation, the specialists will later even come across photos showing abuse in which even animals are involved.

Although there is talk of mutual love in the communication between Blanchard and the women, Blanchard now openly admits that he and other persons are actually responsible for corresponding actions and the distribution of the pictures among themselves. He also gives details of his accomplices. The pictures would have been taken by a woman he only knows under the nickname "VeeGeorge". The third woman in the group uses the pseudonym "AngBank".

These clues are enough for the investigators to finally put them on the right track. Because on one of the incriminating pictures you can see a piece of a badge with a logo. After intensive research, it finally turns out that it is the logo of "Little Ted's" nursery in Plymouth. From then on, the investigators only have to put one and one together to realise that "VeeGeorge" is the nursery teacher Vanessa George. The police do not hesitate a moment longer and arrest the Plymouth woman immediately.

The fallen angel

The private nursery "Little Ted's" will be closed for the time being - and then never reopened. Only in September 2010 will another nursery open in the premises. This time, however, it will be under the control of the local elementary school director and a few trusted persons to ensure the important controls for the protection of the children are present.

In the days following the arrest, a state of emergency prevails in Plymouth: police investigations begin and 313 children from 270 families are initially targeted by the investigators as potential victims. They all had contact with George, who admits to having taken up to eight photos each working day. Eventually, the circle of those affected is condensed to about 30 children. Vanessa George persistently refuses to make concrete statements about her victims or list their names.

At a public meeting on June 9, the shocked inhabitants of Plymouth are informed about the status of the investigation. Everyone is stunned that something like this could have happened in their city and that they not only entrusted Vanessa George with their children, but also liked the abuser so much.

In the following days, the police station's phones break down under the multitude of calls from worried parents. When George is presented to the examining magistrate on

June 10, people outside the courthouse start cursing and spitting at her.

Finally, on June 16, the police are able to identify the woman Blanchard met on Facebook under the name "AngBank". The woman in question is former prostitute, Angela Allen, from Nottingham. The policemen are more than surprised when they discover during the arrest that Allen has made no attempt to destroy evidence - although she already knows about the arrests of her cronies. She also willingly admits that she herself abused a child, took photos of it, and shared them.

July 28, 2009 is a memorable date: On this day, Blanchard and George meet in person for the first time in their lives - when they have to appear in court together. However, it's not until October 1, 2009, before the actual hearing at the Crown Court in Bristol, which is chaired by Judge John Royce, when the three perpetrators will finally stand trial together.

During the trial, all the repugnant actions of the three main antagonists are brought up again. A shocking testimony of how mercilessly the perpetrators of this child pornography circle acted without ever thinking about what they are doing to their helpless victims or their families. A mother will report years later that her child continues to suffer from the incidents. The boy is still wetting his pants at the age of 13, full of anger and aggression.

In addition to the three main perpetrators, two other women are also accused of being part of a paedophile ring; they are Tracy Dawber, a nurse from Southport, Merseyside, and Tracy Lyons, a mother of nine from Portsmouth, Hampshire.

Allen is finally sentenced to at least five years in prison on December 15 2009. When the verdict of nursery teacher Vanessa George is read, the judge takes considerably longer, for he cannot help but express his personal disgust and consternation at her actions. He describes the perpetrator as "evil, cold and calculative" and her deeds would have caused "widespread disgust and incredulity" because they would have revealed "new depths of depravity" and caused a "nationwide shock wave". George is sentenced to at least seven years imprisonment, whereupon it must be thoroughly examined whether she really no longer represents a danger to society after that.

Subsequently, on January 10, 2011, Colin Blanchard is sentenced to at least nine years in prison, and two other members of the paedophile ring receive a minimum sentence of four and seven years in prison.

In the end, many questions remain: How can it be that such horrible crimes are caused by a seemingly trivial internet acquaintance? Did the three of them really only contact each other via Facebook or did they possibly meet in person? And if so: Are there other victims out there - and maybe even more perpetrators?

Since September 18, 2019, these questions have become even more urgent, because after 10 years in prison, Vanessa George is once again at large. Her daughter and ex-husband want nothing more to do with her. Her ex still sees her as a danger to society. In an interview with "The Mirror" he stated that he would be happy if she took her own life. Even though the authorities emphasise that strict conditions apply to George, the parents of the former victims are more than just worried. They are demanding life-long custody to protect other children.

Vanessa George is forbidden to be in areas like Devon and Cornwall. She is also not allowed to have any internet enabled devices. But are these bans enough to protect children from her? She still shows no sign of remorse; until today, people are waiting in vain for her to finally present the list of her victims.

CHAPTER TEN:

The rope awaits her

(by Alexander Apeitos / True Crimes)

"Women murder differently" is a dictum. This is also supported by criminological studies. While men can become violent out of greed, sex, and power, women usually use violence to solve problems and conflicts. Especially when it involves their partner. But while male perpetrators like to boast about the murder, women are usually ashamed of it and are reluctant to talk about it. One of the most extraordinary cases is that of Ruth Ellis, who chooses execution rather than silence.

The beautiful woman is only 28 years old when she is executed on July 13, 1955 as the last woman in Great

Britain to be hanged. A few months earlier, Ruth Ellis had killed her lover, David Blakely, with 6 shots from a revolver.

An act which the public in the stuffy post-war England is enthusiastically looking forward to. The Daily Mail describes the arrest of the young woman as a scene from a classic Hollywood drama: "Six shots from a revolver shook the Easter Sunday calm in Hampstead, and a beautiful platinum blonde stood with her back against the wall". Eagerly, every detail is brought to light to present the good citizens with a story of love and passion, whose leading actress is a "wicked" woman from the red-light milieu.

Ruth Ellis was born as Ruth Neilson on October 9, 1926 in Rhyl, Wales. She is the third of six children of Elisabeth Cothals and Arthur Hornby. At that time, the Roaring Twenties were in full swing. Ruth's mother is a Belgian woman, who fled to Great Britain after the First World War. Arthur Hornby, the father of little Ruth, is an artistic person and works as a musician. For the petty bourgeois family, the crisis is a heavy blow; the parents can only get themselves and their children through with difficulty. Maybe that's why Arthur starts drinking excessively in order to cope with his oppressive everyday life. Because money is tight, and life for the family is hard. When Ruth is 14 years old, she even quits school and

The rope awaits her

starts working as a waitress to help financially support her family.

In 1941, they decide to take a radical step: the whole family move to London. Ruth is just 15 years old and a beautiful teenager. Although the Second World War has been going on for some years, England is still little affected by it. There in the metropolis the family hopes for better job opportunities and a new beginning.

In fact, there will be a new beginning, just two years later. But the events of 1943 will surely turn out completely different than Ruth's parents had dreamed.

They are probably shocked when their 17-year-old daughter confesses to them that she is pregnant. This news is a real drama at a time when a child born out of wedlock is the end of societal standing. This stigmatises the girl, especially since it later turns out that the father has no plans to marry Ruth.

But, at first, the pretty teenager is floating in seventh heaven, because the Canadian soldier who got her pregnant even gets engaged to her. Overjoyed, Ruth gives birth to a little boy, but the happiness does not last long. A short time later, the Canadian comes out with the unpleasant truth that he already has a wife and three children back home. For the young mother, this breach of trust is like a slap in the face and she reacts with a short-circuit action:

Ruth leaves the soldier from overseas and vows that no man will ever succeed in hurting her again.

Now she is on her own and also has to make a living. Therefore, Ruth gives her little boy to her parents and starts working again. What perhaps no one in her family knows at this time, or even suspects: The good-looking Ruth, who has no school-leaving certificate and has not learned any profession, turns the only thing she has into capital - her extraordinary good looks. The 18-year-old earns her money in the flourishing London red-light district, where she probably met the Canadian soldier to begin with. Ruth works as an animation girl in nightclubs, as a nude model, and even as a prostitute. At the beginning of the 50s she gets pregnant by a John, but this time she doesn't indulge in romantic fantasies and aborts the child immediately.

Obviously, Ruth still feels something like the intense desire for a "normal" life. A life with a faithful man, maybe even a little house in the country and a child to watch grow up. Because on November 8, 1950, the surprising happens: Ruth says yes to George Ellis, a dentist she met at a club. For him, it is already the second marriage, and Ruth will soon discover that life at this man's side is anything but normal. Ellis is violent and the marriage is doomed to fail from the very start. Several times Ruth tries to leave George but stays with him - despite the domestic violence.

The young woman gets pregnant quickly. Perhaps she hopes that having a child together will calm the situation. In 1951, their daughter is born. But the child is the end of the marriage because her husband vehemently denies paternity and accuses the ex-prostitute of being unfaithful. Finally, he leaves Ruth and the child. The young woman has no choice but to return to London nightlife.

Once again, Ruth Ellis was humiliated and rejected by a man. The woman who had already sworn never again to be hurt by a man. But she is tough and carries on doggedly - in the one and only environment where she ever got a chance. The attractive blonde is hardworking, determined, and works her way up. In 1953, Ruth Ellis runs her own small nightclub in Knightsbridge, where she also works as a barmaid. And David Blakely comes to this club of all places.

Blakely is 23 years old at this point, 4 years younger than Ruth, who instantly falls for the attractive playboy and racing driver. He is the son of a Scottish doctor from Glasgow and an Irish woman. Although he is sent to a good school, he has only one interest: racing cars. A stormy love story begins between him and Ruth.

Their relationship oscillates between the extremes: David Blakely gets violent with Ruth when he's drunk. But the pretty blonde defends him. Later, she will show off: "He only hit me with fists and hands, but I get bruises very quickly. That's why I was often covered in bruises." Despite the blows, she can't get away from the handsome young man, who also deceives her repeatedly and openly. However, she also has another lover on the side: Desmond Cussen. While Desmond Cussen obviously loves her very much and confesses his love to her again and again, Ruth does not really return his deep affection. She is fixated on Blakely and the down-to-earth Cussen is the complete opposite of him.

But David Blakely eventually loses all interest in Ruth Ellis. He withdraws more and more, and it often leads to arguments, which end in domestic violence. This time, the racer's fury escalates. He strikes Ruth, who is pregnant again at that time, so violently in the abdomen that she suffers a miscarriage.

The young woman is taken to a hospital but is released shortly afterwards. Instead of continuing the episode, David Blakely refuses to accept the blame for beating her and losing her unborn child as a result.

What must have been going on in Ruth Ellis at that moment? Was this the moment when she decided to end her emotional and physical suffering?

On April 10, 1955, Ruth ambushes David Blakely in front of his friends' house. It is Easter Sunday. When he and an acquaintance get into his car, she tries to follow them, but quickly loses sight of them. But chance comes to the woman's rescue: she finally discovers David's car in front of a pub in South Hill Park, Hampstead, North London. Patiently, Ruth waits on the street until Blakely finally leaves the pub. Does she want to give him another chance to explain himself and possibly apologise?

But when he leaves the bar, he ignores his waiting ex-girlfriend, as if he doesn't know her at all. It is probably this behaviour that strengthens Ruth in her plan. She pulls out a Smith & Wesson .38 revolver from her handbag and fires.

The first bullet misses him. It bounces off a house wall and hits an innocent passer-by on the hand.

Another shot!

David Blakely falls to the floor, face down. But he's only injured. Ruth walks up to Blakely, stands over him and fires four more bullets into his back.

But Ruth isn't done yet: she holds the gun to her own head. There are different versions of what follows. While on one hand it is said that she did not have the strength to pull the trigger, on the other hand it is also claimed that the gun jammed. But that puts suicidal tendencies off the table. Finally, as if to confirm it, Ruth shoots the remaining bullets on the floor and instructs David Blakely's acquaintance to call the police.

When the police arrive, Ruth Ellis does not resist arrest. She is still holding the revolver in her hand.

David Blakely dies on the way to the hospital.

Just over two months later, on June 20, 1955, Ruth Ellis' case is heard before the London criminal court Old Bailey - before Judge Cecil Robert Havers and a jury.

The trial is short because the evidence is overwhelming. Especially since there are also witnesses who directly followed the course of events. In this respect the prosecutor asks Ruth Ellis only one question. What was she doing when she shot her victim with the revolver? And Ruth replied with disarming honesty, "It is obvious. When I shot him, I was going to kill him."

Ruth's defence seems to be convinced of her guilt as well. Her attorney doesn't attempt to change her mind or point out exculpatory facts. Rather, he even supports the thesis that the reason for the murder of David Blakely was female hysteria. This is an outdated view, which assumed that hysteria was a neurotic disorder of women, which was partly interpreted as a subtle fight against male superiority. This view has been refuted since the 1980s at the latest.

The rope awaits her

The public prosecutor's office offers Ruth Ellis the option of dropping the murder charge if she pleads guilty to manslaughter. Nevertheless, the young woman, who appears extremely cheerful and relaxed, willingly confesses to the murder of her loved one. If Ruth had accepted this deal, she would not have had the opportunity to tell her version of the events.

It takes just under half an hour for a verdict of guilty. Then the sentence will be announced: Death by hanging.

During her time in prison, Ruth Ellis is said to have seemed very calm and expressionless, perhaps even a little satisfied.

On July 13, 1955, Ruth was executed at 9:00 a.m. by Albert Pierrepoint. Before the trapdoor opened beneath her, she laid her shoulders back and smiled. This is almost a little uncanny for the viewers - what was the woman happy about? Was she hoping to finally be reunited with her beloved David?

This question will remain unanswered forever - as well as another question that will keep the investigators busy far beyond Ellis' death. From whom did she get the murder weapon?

It is widely believed that her second lover, Desmond Cussen, got her the revolver. However, this suspicion could never be proven and Cussen denied the accusation until his death.

In the end, the story of Ruth Ellis is a tragic affair. It is the story of a woman who only wanted to have a better life than the one expected by women at that time, though she didn't stand a chance in her male-dominated world. She repeatedly experienced only violence, humiliation, and abuse - instead of finding the great love and having her own, healthy family. Was she just too naive?

Thomas L. Jones of "Crime Library" will write about her later: "Her misfortune was not that she killed a man. Or that his death resulted in her being the last woman sentenced to death by the rope by the British legal system. The real tragedy is rather that she died for the love of a man who did not deserve it."

Throughout her short life, Ruth Ellis always dreamed of a great change, but she will never know that her death will make a great difference: she will be the last woman to be executed in Britain.

Her conviction moves the public; until shortly before her execution, thousands of people demand a pardon for the young woman. Most of the people of England believe the death penalty to be wrong. The then British Home Secretary receives a flood of angry letters, even a petition for signatures is submitted. Even the judge suggested that the minister should pardon Ellis. But he remains firm in his decision.

In the following years, the laws are finally changed due to the great public outrage.

Ellis' son Adam was sent to a boarding school after his mother was executed; years later he interviewed the prosecutor at his mother's trial. The son is keen to correct the image of his mother. For at that time it was repeatedly claimed that she was a "cold-blooded" person. It is important for Adam to make it clear that this is not true.

In 1982, Adam commits suicide.

Her daughter Georgie also dies of cancer in 2001. Until her death, the author and businesswoman tried to clear her mother's name.

CHAPTER ELEVEN:

A pact among the hopeless

It's a sight that moves you deeply: the bone-white, mighty chalk cliffs of Beachy Head on the English coast. The cliffs rise a good 160 metres steeply above the seemingly endless sea. Only the sky is the limit. This gives Beachy Head a very special flair. The cliff almost looks like a bridge to infinity. And on June 7, 2002, it is exactly that.

When the half-naked body of a young man is found on the stones at the foot of the cliff, it comes as a shock. His body is completely bruised, his bones broken by the impact. He lies there with twisted limbs, wearing only his underpants. A depressing, traumatic sight - even for the police officers who rescue him. In fact, it's a sight they have to endure again and again. Because the headland on the south coast of England, near the town of Eastbourne in East Sussex County, is the highest natural elevation in the country. The combination of height and the mystical aura of the chalk cliffs has made Beachy Head a legendary magnet for suicides.

The young man was in his mid-thirties. At the top of the cliff, the police find his clothes, which he had taken off before the jump, carefully folded and put in a small pile. In the pocket of his jeans the investigators discover a handwritten note: the address of an internet café in London. On the back is a telephone number - but no name. Why was this note so important, why did he carry it with him in his last moments? Could this be a hint to the person who finds it to please inform his relatives?

Obviously, the fall from the chalk cliff killed the young man. But the police officers are faced with many unanswered questions. Did the man really jump to his death? Could it have been a murder that was covered up? Or did he have help in his suicide? Because this has been a criminal act in Britain since the Suicide Act of 1961 and is punishable by law.

Until the 1950s, suicide was a serious offence in England and was severely punished by the authorities. According to public opinion, it was an offence against both God and the King. Whomever survived his suicide was therefore punished. In case of death, the relatives of the suicide could be prosecuted. It was not until the 1950s that the view of the English Church changed on the subject. More and more the idea became accepted that appropriate care by doctors, psychiatrists, and psychologists in combination with drug treatment and general preventive measures is the better alternative. In 1961, the parliament finally passed more modern legislation, which became known as the "Suicide Act". It is, however, a document that betrays the extreme struggle with the subject of suicide, because even when it was passed, the Prime Minister, as well as the Minister of Interior, took opposing positions. With the "Suicide Act", suicide in itself is no longer a punishable offence - with a not insignificant catch! Instead, the second paragraph of the law now defines another criminal offence, namely complicity in suicide. What is meant by this is the support of a life-tired person during suicide, including counselling on how to most effectively deal with suicide.

As punishment of up to 14 years imprisonment is possible. The aim of this new legislation is to prevent murderers from possibly invoking the "Suicide Act". Because without this second paragraph they could always state that they only helped the deceased to commit suicide. Similar laws exist in almost all countries.

Initially, investigators assume that the Beachy Head suicide is the 36-year-old Scotsman Louis Gillies from Glasgow. After all, it is his phone number on the scrap of paper found in the dead man's jeans.

Louis Gillies has successfully completed his studies, is handsome and comes from a wealthy family. But what few people know is that he has mental health problems, is depressed, and has long had suicidal tendencies. Gillies always feels nothing he does is ever good enough. The intense feeling of being a failure is his constant companion. But instead of going to a doctor or psychologist, he seeks closeness with like-minded people. People who have also finished with life and are now looking for a way to take the final step that will end their suffering in this world. Under the nickname "Leander" Gillies is active in the suicide forum of an internet portal.

The website was launched as early as 1987 on what was then "Usenet" as an information portal in which the British founder presented ways to commit suicide. Over time, however, the newsgroup develops into a meeting place for people for whom suicide is seen as a solution to their problems with life. The portal does not see itself as "pro-suicide", but rather as a plea for its own free decision on the subject and the legalization of suicide. With the progress of technical possibilities, chat rooms, sub-pages and mailing lists are quickly emerging. The portal first attracted public attention in September 1992, when one of its users, a computer programmer, actually took his own life and got some suggestions in the forum. Later, the initiator of the forum also commits suicide. In 2016, the platform, which is associated with at least 14 suicide cases, is "frozen"; however, most users are now cavorting in the underground of the Internet, on the Darknet.

When Gillies comes across the Darknet forum, people who would most like to end their lives are exchanging information with each other - about their thoughts, their emotional situation. A particularly important topic is the possibilities of suicide and their respective advantages and disadvantages. What should one consider when "it" is to be done? What should be avoided so that one really "gets the bus"? This formulation is a special kind of "insider" among users, with which suicide is almost lovingly described. Often the members of the newsgroup even cheer themselves on to finally "do it". In this environment, Gillies confesses several times under his nickname "Leander" that the thought of Beachy Head intensely affects him.

On June 5, the user, Leander, posts a notice in the community that "assure-me" got the bus - to Beachy Head. And this, despite "incredible meteorological conditions". The entry is written in an internet café, as can be proven by the IP - on the route from Eastbourne to Glasgow.

Obviously, the experience has excited and stirred Leander a lot, because his lines reveal a real elation and excitement. He even describes the act of suicide as "inspiring, moving, hypnotic". Many in the ASH community, therefore, doubt that Leander ever really wanted to jump. To them, this seems more like the words of a voyeur.

Just one day later, Leander speaks up again in the chat room. This time he explains why he did not manage to end his life as planned. He stresses that the weather irritated him - the rumbling of the sea, the muffled sound of a foghorn, the whistling of the wind. And because of the fog, he could not see the bottom.

It is an oppressive duty for the police to inform the relatives about the suicide. The family's Glasgow residence is quickly located, but when the police ring the doorbell, an unexpected surprise awaits them: a man in his mid-thirties opens it. It is Louis Gillies, who was believed to be dead!

When asked about the events at Beachy Head, the 36-year-old explains without hesitation that he can give details about the suicide. At first, the investigators see the young, educated man as a potential witness, but soon more develops. Because what Gillies tells the police makes the experienced investigators sit up and take notice.

Gillies is also blunt in his statement on the Internet forum, where he is registered under the nickname "Leander". Here he meets the other man, the actual suicide victim of Beachy Head, under the pseudonym "assure-me".

He confesses several times in the forum that the thought of Beachy Head fascinates him - Gillies is the same way. In an entry of November 23, 2001, assure-me describes that he had made a trip to Beachy Head to do "it" - but he backed off at the last minute. He lacks courage at this point. From then on Assure-me also searches the forums for someone to support him in his final action. Someone who will plunge to his death with him to prevent such a procrastination. Since January 2002, the two men have been exchanging emails with each other on a regular basis, topics being their suicidal intentions and the best way to do "it". And they finally get serious - in the period from the end of May to June 7, assure-me, alias Michael Gooden, finally meets Leander at Beachy Head's inn.

As discussed, both men travel to Eastbourne on the appointed day, according to Gillies on June 5, in order to first meet for a joint meal at the "Beachy Head Hotel". For those who are not initiated, it is extremely difficult to imagine this meal. Did the two men finally tell each other their real names on this occasion, or did they remain anonymous to the very end? In view of their imminent death, were they really able to have a relaxed conversation with each other? What did they talk about in those last moments? Did they actually get a bite to eat?

At 8:30 pm the men finally set off for the cliffs; from the hotel it is only a few meters to Beachy Head. The evening is foggy; according to Gillies, they could not even see ten metres ahead of them. As they stand on the cliff edge, they wait a moment. Listening into the silence. The humidity from the sea moves up to them. The fog muffles all the sounds - but then the sudden ringing of a mobile phone rips the approaching night apart.

Gillies takes the call he receives. On the phone is a long-standing friend who suffers from testicular cancer. He's absolutely outraged when he hears what Gillies is up to. Suddenly, the friend does everything he can to talk Gillies out of the story, struggles for him with words. The conversation lasts a whole ten minutes until the 36-year-old Gillies finally agrees not to put his plan into action. Then the caller allegedly asks him to pass the phone on to Gooden to talk to him as well.

But exactly at that moment, according to Gillies' report, he saw the companion's head tip over the cliff. Then, Gooden's body disappeared into the fog. While he was distracted by the call, his companion had jumped to his death.

A pact among the hopeless

Apparently, the police are having a hard time believing Gillies' story. You mean he didn't witness Gooden's leap to his death even though he was standing right there? And the random last-minute phone call also seems fictional to the investigators.

Murder is suspected, which is why Gillies is arrested. Meanwhile, the police begin investigations about the person who was active as assure-me in the ASH-Forum and quickly come across the Londoner, Michael Gooden.

Until 2001, Gooden, lived in the Camberwell district and had no relatives, worked at the post office, and seemed to lead a perfectly normal life. But then there is a radical break, as his former girlfriend Alex St Brice tells the police. What follows now almost seems like a search for meaning: the young man quits his secure job this summer and undertakes an extensive trip to Asia. He travels to Thailand, Vietnam, and Cambodia, only to finally return to England. Alex St Brice, who also lived with Gooden in Camberwell for some time, also reports on an extremely traumatic experience that took place in Thailand. A young woman falls head over heels in love with Gooden, but when he rejects her, she kills herself. The memory of it haunts him. Is that why he has feelings of guilt that he can't deal with?

The news of the suicide of her ex-boyfriend is a heavy blow for St Brice. The young woman is shocked when she receives the news, because she remembers Gooden above all as an incredibly considerate and gentle person, a person without a negative character trait. For her, it is unalterably certain that he could not possibly have committed suicide. Apparently, St Brice didn't know her ex-boyfriend as well as she thinks. During the further investigation of the police it turns out that Gooden in fact suffered from severe depressions and had intense suicide fantasies.

Based on these results, the charge of murder against 36-year-old Gillies is soon dropped, but the complicity in a suicide according to the "Suicide Act" of 1961 is still in play. That's why the 36-year-old Gillies is to be put on trial, despite the severe depression he himself suffers from. This is one of the very first cases in Great Britain in which paragraph 2 of the Suicide Act is applied.

The trial before Lewes Crown Court in Eastbourne is scheduled for April 22, 2003. But the defendant, Louis Gillies, does not appear for the opening. The judge thereupon orders an arrest warrant, which the police are to implement directly. When his colleagues in Glasgow ring at Gillies' front door a few hours later to pick him up, he does not open. There is not a sound to be heard in the family's apartment on Bank Street, a luxurious apartment with a roof terrace. Could Gillies be hiding out to avoid trial? Without further ado, the apartment door is opened by the police, but when they enter, a terrible discovery awaits them: Gillies has hanged himself in his apartment. A suicide note lies next to him.

Did the court case and the strong public pressure finally cause Gillies to decide to "take the bus" after all? A tragic development - but possibly the only conceivable solution for him.

Countless questions remain unanswered: How is it possible that talented, attractive young men who have their whole lives ahead of them choose suicide as their only way out? Why did they have the impression that they had nothing to live for? And how much blame does the disastrous Internet portal with its countless tips and instructions bear for their death?

CHAPTER TWELVE:

The surrogate family

The 10th of May 2009 seems to be a beautiful spring day. Ideal for fishing. Therefore, the two anglers decide to spend a relaxing day at the "Blue Lagoon", a pond in Arlesey, Bedfordshire. This pond is in the east of England, near the towns of Stevenage and Luton. Since the quarry was closed in the early 1930s, and the pits filled with water, the water area, idyllically situated between extensive meadows and fields, has been a popular destination for excursions and a good fishing ground. But there is nothing idyllic about what the two fishing friends will find on this day.

When they arrive at the bank, they discover an overturned wheelbarrow in the shallow water. Next to it is a big pile of plastic. At first, the men are simply annoyed at the discarded waste. They decide to pull the wheelbarrow and the pile of plastic ashore. But the closer they get, the more the two anglers get the feeling that something is not quite right. The feeling suddenly turns into pure panic when they finally realise what is floating in the water - a human torso!

The Hertfordshire police, who are alerted immediately, retrieve the large carrier bag from the shallow water. A mutilated, headless torso emerges, showing signs of violence on both the front and the back. It is suspected that the wheelbarrow was used to transport the remains to the lake. Since the body is already bloated and there is also wrinkled "wash skin", the police officers are sure that it must have been lying in the lake for several days. Most likely weighted down with something to keep the body under water. The so-called "wash skin" is a phenomenon that is typical of floaters. The puffy appearance is because in the complete absence of air, body fat is converted into fat wax, which then surrounds the body shape like a shell.

During the search, the police also discover the victim's hands and feet. The deceased is identified as Michael Gilbert. The young man lived in Blackburn, Lancashire, but also had connections to Cambridge and King's Lynn in Norfolk. The head remains missing.

The Hertfordshire police are searching for the

murderer at full speed over the next few days, and even a mobile police station will be opened at Blue Lagoon and numerous search posters will be put up.

The forensic examination reveals further shocking facts, although the already advanced state of decomposition does not allow the exact cause of death to be determined. The decapitation involved cutting the soft tissue of the neck and aorta with a knife. There is a stab wound to the chest, where an artery was cut, and several internal injuries were inflicted. There are also two other stab wounds. Furthermore, there are internal injuries in the stomach and intestines, and there are air rifle pellets under the skin in the lower back.

Only a short time later, the police initially announce that five people have been arrested. A few days later, two more are arrested.

Michael Gilbert was born in 1982 as the third of five children. Unfortunately, his family was anything but a shelter of security and so, the cheerful boy with the chubby face and the big glasses grows up partly in children's homes. Most of his siblings have a similar situation. In 1993, his sister accuses Michael, who was just 11 years old at the time, of having sexually molested her. This incident is probably the one that will influence his character for a long time. From this point on, the boy is stigmatised. At school, he is the victim of bullying, especially after a breast is removed at the age of 13.

When Michael is once again in a home in 1998, he meets young James Watt there, whom he joins. He has criminal potential and both commit several crimes together. In the year 2000, both are well-known to the police and are convicted several times. Michael already had obvious psychological problems at that time.

His younger brother, Chrissy, will later suspect that Michael was such an easy victim for James Watt at the age of 15, because the long time in the home of his own family would have alienated him completely. The teenager grows up to be a very vulnerable and naive young man, whom others can exploit with playful ease. The only constant in his life is the contact to James Watt. Fatally.

After his time in the home, Gilbert maintains contact with James Watt - until his death. In 2006, Michael will even call himself a part of the family.

The multi-headed Watt family is notorious throughout Luton. Based on relevant experience, they are either called, "Luton's most notorious anti-social neighbours" or a "caricature of the neighbours from hell". Most of the family members have no occupation and are known for their violence and criminal acts. Again and again they change homes, with neighbours complaining by default

The surrogate family

that the peace and quiet is over as soon as the Watts appear. Neighbours report that the Watts carry baseball bats and knives and claim that this is "for their own protection". They cause noise and are considered dirty and unkempt. One neighbour even feels compelled to install a surveillance camera, as the Watts repeatedly come to the family's property in his absence to stare at his wife and daughter through the windows. In 2001, the police visited the family 112 times.

The list of criminal acts committed by individual family members is impressive: in 2009, James Watt (27) had 14 convictions for 22 different crimes, including assault and shooting at people with an air rifle. His brother Robert (20) has two convictions, including theft. James' girlfriend, Natasha Oldfield (29), mother of two, has committed robberies; Nichola Roberts (21), Richard Watt's partner, can even "shine" with four convictions and one bail, each time she has filled petrol up without paying. Only the matriarch of this clan, Jennifer Smith-Dennis (58), has a clean slate legally until 2009.

It is this family of all people that Michael Gilbert chooses as a surrogate family. The following ten years must have been like hell on earth, because he is kept like a slave by the Watts and forced to work for them. Several times the deeds are even recorded on video: There is evidence of

Michael being cut with a knife and beaten with a baseball bat. But he is also kicked and struck with billiard balls. There are also documents of someone shooting at the young man with an air rifle, of him drinking his own urine or being made to stand in boiling water. Pit bulls are set upon the 26-year-old or he is forced to tease one of the family's big lizards with a stick until it finally attacks him.

The girlfriend of his "friend" James Watt, who is also the one who torments Michael the most, even invents a game she calls "Game Show". Here, people who torture Gilbert receive prize money - graded according to severity. Oldfield lists in her diary not only the "winning amounts" (5 pounds per slap, 10 pounds for a boxing punch, 15 pounds for a kick and 25 pounds awarded for a headbutt) but also ideas for further game shows. Apparently, the family saw the young man's treatment as a form of "entertainment".

But Gilbert is not only for entertainment, he is also a kind of cash cow, as he often has to hand over his welfare payments to them. So, it's no wonder that they do their utmost to find him when he leaves. The Watts are amazingly clever at this: James Watt contacts the Department for Work and Pensions and, knowing Gilbert's national security number, pretends to be him. This way they can find out where Gilbert last received and signed his payments. There they go and bring him back

The surrogate family

to Luton - sometimes even by force. However, Gilbert sometimes comes back to them of his own free will.

A fact that is difficult to understand. Especially since Gilbert's sister is Watts' girlfriend for a while before Oldfield and even lives with him. She even watches her brother being attacked and abused. Furthermore, the local police also know that Gilbert could be in trouble. However, they don't follow up on this because he, the victim, says on one occasion that this "would only make things worse in the long run".

When Gilbert suffers a stab wound and is shot at with an air rifle in January 2002, someone in his family reports this to the police. Because the Watts don't call back on request and Gilbert doesn't show up for an appointment at the station, the incident fizzles out.

Later on, an expert report by the IPCC, the Independent Police Complaints Commission, will therefore state that investigators suspect that Gilbert was faking his injuries.

In fact, the young man probably did not visit a hospital the entire time, despite how painful the injuries sometimes were. There are no records of this in the clinics.

And when Gilbert is kidnapped by James Watt in June 2007 in front of a friend in Cambridge, and in January 2008 in the presence of his brother's girlfriend, the alarmed police do not react consistently and finally let the matter rest.

At the end of 2008, the Watts think up a new torture method for Gilbert. They now do sit ups - but since they need a little thrill, they lean on a piece of wood lying over Michael's mouth and jump around on his stomach. One of the "participants" is Robert Watt, who weighs a good 133 kilos. Afterwards, Gilbert is in extreme pain, loses control of his bowels, and is hardly able to walk. Nevertheless, nobody takes him to a hospital.

A dry, concise entry in Oldfield's diary of game show ideas and rules can be found in the night of January 21-22, 2009: "Gilbert ends up dead."

Perhaps it is now dawning on the Watt family that it will end unhappily if they are associated with this death. That's probably why they decide to dump him secretly in Blue Lagoon. And so that no one can determine his identity, the body is chopped up into pieces and the parts are disposed of in separate bags. They wrap the torso in several layers of garbage bags and kitchen foil and then put it into a large DIY bag. They then place the remains of Michael Gilbert in the trunk of Robert Watts' car to take them to the lake in Arlesey. For the approximately 1.6-kilometre journey, they first use a fishing cart and then a wheelbarrow. With a large stone from the garden of the

The surrogate family

Watts' house, the parcel with the torso is weighted down and sunk into the water, with the hopes that the body will remain that way.

When it is known that the corpse found in the lake is Michael Gilbert, the police can quickly make the connection to the Watts family based on the data they already have - and finally become active. In the short term, a total of seven members of the clan are arrested and questioned. As Richard Watt agrees to support the police in their investigations, the head of Michael Gilbert is finally found on February 4, 2010. Four weeks later, the trial against the "Neighbours from Hell" begins at Luton Crown Court for the murder of Gilbert.

At the trial, which will be presided over by Judge John Bevan, further details of Gilbert's abuse will be discussed. Witness Philipp Budd, who is a regular guest at the Watts, reports that the young man had to wear a collet on his genitals so that he could be led around on a leash like a dog. Furthermore, since 2008, he had been dressed only in boxer shorts to make sure that he would not run away again.

23-year-old Zoe Smith, a friend of Colin Watt's, says she saw Gilbert being chained to a bunk bed with handcuffs on his feet, where she and Colin slept. According to her, she has entered the family home about 150 times over the course of her three year relationship with Colin Watt and almost every time Gilbert has been abused and tortured in some way.

Colin Watt testifies that he moved out of his parents' home some time before Gilbert was killed. The increasing violence against Gilbert was the reason: "It made me nauseous. I thought I couldn't take it anymore, I had to go." After the disastrous events of the night of 21-22 January, Colin Watt received a phone call from his brother Robert telling him to come home and that he needed to tell him something. The news was shocking: "Robert said, 'We killed Michael.' - I walked out and could only cry."

In April, the verdict is finally passed: James Watt, his girlfriend Natasha Oldfield, and Nichola Roberts, the girlfriend of his brother Richard, are found guilty of the murder of Michael Gilbert. They receive 36, 18, and 15 years imprisonment. Richard Watt, Robert Watt, and his mother Jennifer Smith-Dennis are found guilty of murder in the family and are sentenced to 6, 8, and 10 years in prison. They are also found guilty of attempting to obstruct justice. Only the 70-year-old father, Antonio Watt, is acquitted on all counts.

Judge Bevan describes the whole thing as a "grotesque story", Gilbert died a "cruel, lonely and brutal death" and to call him a slave is a "mild understatement". James Watt, who was the leader of the deeds, is described by him as "dangerous, cruel, vindictive, malicious and heartless" - obviously an apt characterization, because when James Watt's sentence was pronounced, one hears him say, "Cheers!"

The judge also informs the members of the jury that they are relieved from further jury duty for life because they had to endure listening to all these horrible things.

At first, Michael Gilbert's mother Rosalie White (49) doesn't want to comment on all this, but after the trial she gives vent to her anger and desperation. Her rage is mainly directed against the mother of the Watt brothers: "What kind of woman allows such things to happen in her house? And for all this time? You raise your children so that they develop to the best of their ability - but not so that they become cold-blooded murderers. This mother could have helped Michael, but she did nothing."

Subsequently, due to years of inactivity by the authorities in the Michael Gilbert case, investigations by the Luton Safeguarding Of Vulnerable Adults Board as well as the Independent Police Complaints Commission (IPCC) are carried out. In their reports, published in 2011, both uncover various errors and dramatic misjudgements committed by different authorities. Michael Gilbert's life could have been saved.

In May 2011, Richard Watt's sentence will be reduced to four years for his assistance in the police investigation. The appeals of Watt, Oldfield, and Roberts are rejected.

A statement made by Richard Watt during the trial casts a tragic light on why the mentally unstable, naive young man endured all those years of abuse and torture. When Richard asked, "Why do you put up with all this?" Gilbert simply replied, "Because I love you so much, you are my family."

CHAPTER THIRTEEN:

Brazilian preferences

When the racy Brazilian Roselane Nonato looks at the notice in the window of the newsagent, she is immediately interested. A lady from North London is looking for a cleaning lady because she does not have enough time herself. Perfect, the slender, attractive woman with the long black hair and a complexion tanned by the South American sun is probably thinking and looking for a pen at this moment. She notes down the contact details and will call the number shortly afterwards. Because Roselane Nonato, whose last name has recently changed to Driza, is urgently looking for a job. And she would do anything for that. Anything.

The then 29-year-old Brazilian, who is said to have studied philosophy for a time in her home country, entered Great Britain in 1998 on a tourist visa. However, it is only valid for six months and Roselane Nonato may be planning to stay longer.

Only a few weeks after her arrival, the first unexpected turn in her new life comes: in a nightclub she meets Mane Driza, a muscular, somewhat hulking man with a bald head and bull's neck, who claims to have fled from Kosovo; in England he asks for asylum. The two fall in love and marry shortly afterwards. However, Roselane Driza's new husband disappears unexpectedly shortly after the wedding. It turns out that Mane Driza is a member of the Albanian mafia and has killed a fellow countryman in England. Therefore, the man, who is often called "Tony Montana" (the name of Al Pacino in the mafia movie "Scarface") by acquaintances of the scene, disappears from the island without further ado. Later on, it turns out that he is actually a wanted serial killer.

The abandoned wife doesn't know anything about this. When her tourist visa finally expires, she manages to get a residence permit as a student. But she does not enrol in any university. A return to Brazil is also out of the question. In order to earn a living, Driza begins looking for a job and finally introduces herself to Judge J. at the newspaper vendor's notice board. The twice married mother of two children is in her 50s and hires the Brazilian as a cleaning lady.

At this time, J. lives with a colleague, Judge Mohammed Ilyas Khan (52 years old). The divorced father of two has been in office since 1968 and, like J., with whom he is currently having an affair, works as a judge at the Tribunal for Asylum and Immigration. With his grey hair and thick, grey full beard, the man with the dark, stern eyes almost looks a little like an ageing lion. Both he and judge J. decide on cases every day, whether they concern justified or unjustified applications for asylum, right of residence, legal and illegal immigration and also expulsions. Even though they are so closely involved in these matters, when J. hires Roselane, she does not ask whether she has a valid residence permit or whether she is registered with the relevant authorities. Nor does she ask whether she has a national insurance number.

Shortly after Driza took up her duties, the affair of the two judges ended and they separated. Ilyas Khan is looking for his own apartment and Driza now starts to keep his new domicile in order as well.

Surprisingly, both immigration judges employ an illegal immigrant. An offence punishable by up to two years in prison and a fine of £2,000. Both later claim they had no idea that Driza was in England illegally. Obviously, amazingly enough, they also had no idea to ask the Brazilian woman about it.

Finally, J. fires her cleaning lady, but she consoles herself in a very special way: first, she sends a letter to the Department for Constitutional Affairs, in which she states that J. has employed her without a work permit. Furthermore, the sexy Brazilian woman starts an affair with 52-year-old Ilyas Khan. The older man is in seventh heaven and completely in love with his new companion, who is 23 years younger than him. He describes Driza as "real chilli-hot stuff" and praises her extraordinary sexual abilities in an e-mail. The fact is: The judge in love not only hires an illegal immigrant, but also starts an affair with her.

In November 2000, Driza's residence permit as a student expires, but for her this is no reason to leave Great Britain. In return, no official attempt is made to track her down or send her back to Brazil.

Roselane Driza has already acclimatised so well that she gives good advice to other illegals. Among other things, her advice is proven: "Present yourself as a victim - exaggerate, pretend to be depressed and you can get everything. The people in this country are so gullible." Furthermore, the attractive dark-haired girl boasts that she even managed to have her eyes and nose done by a plastic surgeon.

The Brazilian is doing extremely well for herself. In the meantime, she has moved in with Ilyas Khan full time. At some point, she discovers some private videos that attract her attention. Driza is immediately electrified by what was recorded on the tape and she smells a chance. Because you can see Ilyas Khan and Judge J. playing wild sex games. But that's not all: Judge J. is also seen snorting cocaine. And Ilyas Khan is not only with her but also with another woman - a mysterious blonde. Struck by an idea, Driza takes the video.

The cleaning lady is trying to blackmail the two judges: she demands 20,000 pounds from them if they want the two videos back. On the other hand, Driza wants to inform the Lord Chancellor, one of the highest and most important dignitaries in the government, that she works for the two judges and both of them know that she is here illegally.

But Judge J., who is now having an affair with Judge N. and who calls Driza a "fucking Brazilian bitch", will not go along with the blackmail. Neither does Ilyas Khan. They both turn in their Brazilian cleaning lady instead.

But what follows is even more astonishing. For despite the charges, Ilyas Khan apparently has no intention of parting with his "sexy pearl" - when Driza is arrested, she still lives in his apartment. Everybody would also expect that the two judges would now face countless hearings and disciplinary sanctions - but far from it! Despite the misconduct, neither of them will be suspended. Judge J. is instead taking sick leave and thus continues to receive her full annual salary of 117,680 pounds.

The trial in Old Bailey in London also comes as a surprise. After just 6 days of trial, Judge Beaumont's verdict is passed: 33 months in prison for the now 37-year-old Roselane Driza. She is sentenced to 30 months for blackmailing Judge J. Regarding Ilyas Khan, there is no blackmail, he has at least let the woman continue living with him. However, Driza is convicted of stealing two videos in connection with him. This will get her another three months in prison. The judge also recommends that the woman be deported. Because Judge J. was a victim of blackmail, she is allowed to keep her anonymity. Judge Mohammed Ilyas Khan, on the other hand, merely says that his bad behaviour is the cause of his dilemma. He is denied anonymity. However, both judges otherwise get off scot free.

Judge Beaumont describes Driza as a "greedy and determined woman" in the grounds of his judgement. Although her annoyance about the dismissal by J. may be justified, this is not the real reason for her action. Driza saw an opportunity to get a lot of money and took it. The fact that she was unsuccessful in her blackmailing efforts is considered as a mitigating factor. However, the theft of the tapes is to be seen as an attempt to gain power over their owner, Ilyas Khan, just in case.

When Roselane Driza leaves the Old Bailey that day and is taken to the cells, she throws a kiss and smiles at the waiting journalists. She has every reason to do so, as the appeal proceedings in 2007 will show.

What surprises many is that Mohammed Ilyas Khan is not even present at the sentencing in the Old Bailey - he is himself a judge at the Feltham Tribunal that day and has to decide on cases of other immigrants.

After the trial, Amtul Khan, the divorced wife of Ilyas Khan, speaks out for the first time. She emphasises that she has broken off all contact with her ex-husband and that the rest of his family, and two siblings, do not want to know him.

Judge J. is on sick leave for the entire 18 months of the investigation against Driza and the subsequent trial. During this time, she continues to draw her salary of about 142,300 Euros per year, which amounts to 246,000 Euros for the 18 months. On December 31 2006, J. took early retirement on account of her state of health and has been drawing early pensions ever since.

In July 2007, the convicted Brazilian woman is finally released on appeal, as the retrial is stopped by the Crown

Prosecution Service. Both judges involved are too ill to testify, therefore an acquittal is ruled for lack of evidence.

The Office for Judicial Complaints, however, initiates a 19-month investigation into the employment of Roselane Driza by the two judges. The focus here is mainly on Ilyas Khan. In May 2008, the result against the judge will be officially announced: that Ilyas Khan has shown "poor judgment" in not checking Roselane Driza's employment status. However, he is allowed to keep his job with an annual salary of a good 133,300 euros and he will not be deprived of his later annual pension of 57,600 euros plus a lump sum of at least 120,000 euros.

Since the end of the investigation, Ilyas Khan has also been on permanent sick leave. Usually, this means that, after your company sick pay runs out, you will only receive the statutory sickness benefit provided by the government. At an advanced age, early retirement is often under discussion. Neither of these things happens with Ilyas Khan.

In 2009, something unexpected happens: One day after Ilyas Khan finally retires at the age of 64, he dies.

Again, two years later there is news from Roselane Driza; the Brazilian is finally deported on February 23, 2011 and goes back to her home country.

CHAPTER FOURTEEN:

Dangerous love affair

When 32-year-old Tony Charlton sets off from Huddersfield to Midgley near Wakefield on May 23, 2001, the owner of two printshops is in high spirits. He is happy to take on the 80-kilometer route to pick up his four-year-old daughter, Amy.

He misses his little Amy very much and is happy when he finally arrives at the house of Daniel O'Brien, a listed feudal building with a value of about 300.000 Euro. On his bell, Charlton's ex-wife Janet opens the door. She is an attractive, slender blonde with ample breasts, who wears her long hair conspicuously ash-blond. She has clear blue eyes, with which she looks at you in a slightly demanding and provocative way. Something that drives all the men crazy. Especially in combination with the celebratory smile that likes to play around the corners of her mouth.

The 36-year-old woman seems completely calm and relaxed. While she calls their daughter, she chats about the fact that they just went for a walk in the park together. When Amy finally arrives, Janet calls Daniel upstairs to say goodbye to the four-year-old. When there is no answer, Janet asks her daughter to go upstairs and say goodbye to Daniel O'Brien. But strangely enough, she refuses. So, her mother takes her by the hand and the two of them go upstairs together into the bedroom.

Tony, who is waiting downstairs, becomes stiff with fright as the horrible screams and sobbing begin. He hurries up the stairs, meeting his hysterically screaming and crying ex-wife who runs outside the door. Confused, Tony Charlton enters the room and holds his breath in horror. "A massacre!" it shoots through his head. "This is a real massacre!"

The numerous mirrors in the master bedroom of Woodside Hall, Old Wood Yard, reflect the same horrible image a thousand times over: the blood-soaked corpse of millionaire Daniel O'Brien, whose skull contains a fireman's axe measuring a good 60 cm! And like some kind of perverse jewellery, a suspender belt with a leopard print pattern and white fishnet tights hang from it.

But that's not all: The Yorkshire tycoon apparently died a horrible death in the middle of an intimate bondage game. For the position of the hacked-up body indicates that Daniel must have been naked, handcuffed, kneeling - before his "mistress"? Because his eyes are blindfolded and, in his mouth, there is a rubber ball, which was secured with a dog collar. A huge bull whip lies on the bed.

The coroner also discovers the marks on the dead man's back. The bondage left him completely defenceless when the axe blows fell on him. The killer struck twenty times in all, striking the head and shoulders. Finally, the axe remained stuck in the head of the helpless man.

Despite or perhaps because of the extreme horror of his ex-wife when she discovers the body of her new life partner, Tony Charlton is astonished. Because in retrospect she does not seem to mourn him. After a week, he is sure: Only his ex-wife can be the murderer!

Meanwhile, Janet assures the police investigators that she has nothing to do with the murder. She visits the morgue where Daniel O'Brien is laid out, places lilies on his body and a family photo. She then tells O'Brien's mother, the 72-year-old pensioner, Elisabeth, that he looked better than he did when he was alive. She also confides to the pensioner that she lives in great fear. She fears that she and her daughter could become the next victims of the killer.

The investigators are even more surprised when Janet Charlton turns up at the police station six weeks after the murder, accompanied by a lawyer. She confesses that it was her who killed the millionaire. But it was self-defence, because the businessman had threatened her and said he wanted to kill her and her daughter.

But how did all this happen?

Born in Oldham, she moved to Huddersfield at the age of 18 where she obtained her degree in Business Studies. She then worked in the recruitment department of a temporary employment agency. At this time, the 25-year-old meets Tony Charlton, who is four years younger at the time. Although Janet is in a relationship, she begins an affair with Tony on the very first night. He confesses that he found her incredibly sexy and the thought of having sex with an older woman excited him to no end. These secret meetings continue for quite a while until Tony realises that he has fallen in love with the blonde. And her adventurous background only makes her even more attractive to the young, naive man - because according to a list she had sex with about 115 men before she met him!

Two and a half years later the two get married in Mauritius. Everything seems wonderful until 1997 when daughter Amy is born. Tony, whose print shops are flourishing, is in heaven - but for Janet it is the starting signal to go to parties and have fun. It's as if she wanted to prove that the little child will not change her life. When Amy is nine months old, the marriage is finally over. Janet goes hunting for men once more – and when she sleeps with the married neighbour, Tony finally applies for a divorce. In 1998, the divorce is final, and the deal is extremely advantageous for Janet Charlton: She gets a house, a car, a high monthly alimony for Amy, and a generous severance pay, from which she gets new breasts, among other things.

Now the blonde is finally free again and sleeps with anyone she feels like. She works for an escort service where she can be hired for about 200 € per hour. Through this internet escort service Charlton meets the rich businessman Daniel O'Brien in 2000. He is a fan of hardcore pornography, which supposedly extends to bestiality

Just four weeks after they met, Charlton and her daughter Amy move in with O'Brien. And the businessman is going to catapult their sex life to a whole new level: from now on there will be sex with strangers in public, orgies, and they will attend swinger parties.

It takes just eight months, then O'Brien seems to get tired of the blonde. On May 22, he admits that he has rekindled the affair with one of Janet's predecessors;

he had sex with her in the park of Chatsworth House in Derbyshire. He may have been planning to break up with Charlton. Just 24 hours after that revelation, O'Brien is dead. with his skull split in two.

The story is a staple for the British press. In the following months, Janet Charlton is stylised in the media as a female demon because she fulfils every cliché: she is a murderer, she is blonde, and apparently loves sex.

In the spring of 2002, the trial begins at Leeds Crown Court, presided over by Judge Norman Jones. During the trial, Charlton admits to the murder, but she emphasises that it was an act of self-defence. According to Charlton, O'Brien had sexually used and humiliated her for several years, raped and beaten her repeatedly. She also said she was forced by him to have sex with several men at once in a club. Furthermore, she had to have sex with him in public parking lots.

During this public "confession", those present were deeply immersed in deviant sexual preferences. For example, this is how the "dogging" and "picking" scene becomes known to the public. Because apparently O'Brien and Charlton were part of it. Dogging is about sex in public, especially in cars in public parking lots or in the open air - and that is when there are children next door with their mothers in the playground, people having picnics or the like. With her own partner, but also with other partners. Often friends of the "picking" - they enjoy watching sexual intercourse in public.

Charlton confesses that she had at least 60 lovers during this time. She had once been in a sauna with ten men alone, while O'Brien watched.

The blonde woman stresses that she was allegedly forced to do these actions. She would have felt humiliated and stupid. Finally, O'Brien threatened her and told her that he had already killed several children - which she believed immediately. When he finally announced that he would rape Amy and cut off her head, she lived in constant fear for herself and her daughter. And she explains emphatically: "He is an abysmally evil man and has killed children before. I know for a hundred percent that he would have killed Amy if I hadn't killed him first."

In her distress, she allegedly wanted to calm the businessman down with sex, but then her eyes fell on the axe that was standing in the bedroom. When he was blindfolded, gagged, and tied on his knees, she struck O'Brien several times. How many times, she doesn't remember. She explains, "I didn't know what I was doing - I only regained consciousness when I saw blood on my foot and wiped it off."

Meanwhile, her daughter was playing downstairs in the garden.

Still numb, Charlton showered and put on clean clothes. Then she and her daughter went to the park. And in that time, every memory of the killing disappeared from her mind. She affirms several times that she could remember absolutely nothing. She's just glad that Amy didn't see any of it.

A neuropsychiatrist confirms that Janet Charlton's report about an amnesia regarding the murder is quite plausible. Other witnesses say she was a victim of "Battered Woman Syndrome". This is a phenomenon known since the 1990s, in which women who have been severely pressured and humiliated by their partner can literally "freak out" and then kill them violently, because otherwise they see no possibility of escaping this relationship.

However, the extremely unemotional description of the murder by the perpetrator makes several observers of the trial feel uneasy. Especially since Janet Charlton does not express any regret about the crime, but rather declares: "I did the right thing - and I will say so for all eternity. This man was crazy."

For the prosecution, however, it is clear that the motive for the murder is simply revenge and jealousy, because O'Brien obviously wanted to end the relationship in order to start over with a former partner. Concerning Janet Charlton, the assessment of the public prosecutor Paul Worsley is: "She is a heartless murderer and perfect actress."

However, they all agree on one thing: Daniel O'Brien was an extremely problematic personality, who lived out any sexual preference without any consideration for loss. Judge Norman Jones will describe him as follows in his opinion: that he was "a flawed man with extremely depraved sexual proclivities." And Janet Charlton, with her extremely relaxed attitude to sexuality - if not a tendency towards nymphomania - was more than willing to indulge in these particular practices. Furthermore, the judge describes O'Brien as a control freak who did everything to cut Charlton off from her previous life and separate the daughter from her father.

This is certainly the reason why the verdict, which was handed down in May 2002 after 19 hours of deliberation over four days, was relatively mild. According to the jury, while self-defence is ruled out from the outset because of O'Brien's bondage, the facts of the murder do not align with the evidence. For obviously there was no premeditation on Charlton's part. Rather, the woman had completely lost her self-control and in her rage, she had attacked the man with an axe. Therefore, the sentence is murder in the heat of passion and a prison term of five years is imposed.

When Charlton is led out of the courtroom, she cries and shapes the word "Sorry" with her mouth towards her parents sitting in the gallery.

For Daniel's mother, Elisabeth O'Brien, the sentence comes as a shock. She cannot understand how a mother can send her child into the bedroom when there is a corpse covered in blood up there. For her, it is also "outrageous" that the axe is said to have already been in the bedroom.

Tony Charlton will mention to the press a month after the verdict that his daughter Amy admitted in an interview with some social workers that she saw much more than what was assumed. During the interview, the little girl says she saw her mommy hit Daniel with a big stick.

As the axe blade penetrated the businessman's skull, Amy heard loud noises coming from the bedroom - so loud that even the ceiling was shaking. The girl runs up the stairs and screams "Mommy" loudly as the axe falls on Daniel. At that moment, Janet's anger subsides, and she begins to cry. Charlton shows the child out of the room and says they are going to the park as a reward. Then she makes the girl promise not to say anything. Janet Charlton claims that Amy didn't see anything - but the girl tells her father about red spots on the carpet and that Daniel looked so different. And she does not want to see her mother again.

Is this all just one little girl's fantasy?

In an appeal process, the sentence for Janet Charlton is reduced from the original five years to three and a half. In total, the blonde woman will eventually spend less than two years in prison. After 18 months, she leaves the open prison in Askham Grange. She will first move to her parents in Middleton but wants to leave everything behind as she stresses to the media. After a bitter legal battle over daughter Amy, Tony now has sole custody.

For his mother, Charlton is simply a "selfish and manipulative woman". And she insists that no one deserves to die the way Daniel O'Brien did.

CHAPTER FIFTEEN:

The Good Samaritan

Months later, the entire family is still numb from the events of September 28, 2008. Especially after the verdict, which must have felt like a slap in the face. The younger brother, Kevin McGarahan, cannot bear the memories associated with Frank in almost every place in the city of Norwich. Everything reminds him of that horrible night. And so, the family are already thinking of moving somewhere else to finally put it all behind them.

Frank McGarahan was born in 1963 and grew up in modest circumstances; his father is a carpenter. In the high school he attends in Battersea, South London, the friendly boy with the rounded face and wide eyes quickly gains a reputation as a peacemaker. While others stand around yelling and cheering at their opponents in the schoolyard during fierce fights, possibly cheering them on by clapping their hands, Frank always defuses such situations. This is easy for him, because his schoolmates already then attest to his disarming personality and natural authority.

It is not surprising that after high school, Frank McGarahan began law studies at Southampton University, which he successfully completed in 1985. He then joined Deutsche Bank, before finally moving to Barclays Capital, where he climbed the career ladder and became head of Barclays Wealth. He manages assets of almost 1.6 billion euros across 21 countries, overseeing around 7,700 employees and hundreds of investors.

Frank McGarahan also does well in his private life: in 1999 he marries the three-year younger stewardess, Alison Ogden, with whom he moves into a spacious house in a Hertfordshire village near Much Hadham. Their happiness is finally rounded off by their two daughters, first-born Nancy, and then Grace, born in June 2008.

There is only one thing he regrets: he has too little time for his family. When his second daughter Grace is born, McGarahan is seriously considering reducing his workload and changing his lifestyle significantly.

Because Frank is a true family man, it is only natural for him to drive the 130 kilometres or so to Norwich in

The Good Samaritan

East Anglia on Saturday September 27, 2008 to attend the baptism of his niece Thea the following Sunday. After all, she is the very first child of his youngest brother. After a family dinner, Frank, his brother Kevin, and their cousin Sean Ryan decide to celebrate. The three men and two women enjoy a few drinks on a tour of the bars in the city centre. It is not until shortly before 3 a.m. that they decide to end the evening. Together they make their way to the taxi stop at Guildhall Hill, where they queue up and wait their turn. But before their taxi arrives, Frank McGarahan discovers something that alarms him.

At a distance of just under 200 metres, a group of young people attack a man, the 35-year-old Lithuanian Robertas Sinkevicius; in some comments there is later talk of up to 12 people. From a distance, the man is initially mistaken for a homeless man. Some passers-by address the gang, but without success.

When the efforts of the other passers-by fail, Frank McGarahan sets off and goes to the highly aggressive group of young drunkards to settle the dispute. He cannot possibly stand by and watch an innocent man get beaten up by a mob. The 46-year-old does not think about it any further, it is simply his duty as a human being to prevent anyone from being seriously injured. But he will pay a terrible price for his moral courage.

Kevin and Sean share his attitude and follow Frank to the young men. As there are several surveillance cameras installed at this place, their recordings later on prove that the trio approach carefully and don't show any signs of aggressive behaviour.

According to Sean, the three are received by the youths, including Ben and Tom Cowles (22 and 21), with savage insults. However, the aggressive young men later state on record that they simply told the trio: "You don't know what he has done. He got what he deserved." Kevin's reply follows on his heels: "You are cowards. You should be ashamed of yourselves, messing with someone walking alone."

Having to be called cowards obviously does not suit the young people at all. They scream back in rage:

"It's got fucking nothing to do with you! Fuck off, or you'll get some too!"

Then the young men suddenly attack the trio, that actually only wants to settle the quarrel, provide peace, and avoid the worst. The surveillance videos document every detail that follows. First, Ben Cowles, without any warning, makes a violent punch to the head of banker McGarahan, who goes down like a log. Then he takes his brother Kevin into the headlock and punches his head several times. After a fierce punch, the banker goes down as well. Tom Cowles enters the surprising fight shortly after him and also attacks the McGarahan brothers. He attacks Frank who is trying to get up on his hands and knees. He steps on him and gives him numerous brutal boxing blows. Another young man, Daniel Moy, also enters the fight and sends his surprised cousin Sean Ryan to the ground.

Frank McGarahan manages to get back on his feet again. He stands there swaying - only to suddenly collapse. Then he lies motionless on his back.

Besides the surveillance videos, there is also an eyewitness of the violent attack. Darryl Lawton, the doorman of a nearby strip club, hears the noise of the fight as the young people attack the homeless Sinkevicius. He also runs to help. But when he arrives, the attack on the McGarahan brothers and their cousin is already in full swing.

He sees two men lying on the ground and the attackers coming at them with fists. For Lawton, it is a case of extreme brutality, as if all inhibitions had been removed from the attackers who simply want to destroy their victims. One of the young men is put in a headlock by the doorman, but he has to let go because he has the support of a comrade, whose kicks break Lawton's jaw. Then the young people all run away - and two men lie unconscious on the street: the homeless Sinkevicius and Frank McGarahan.

Lawton, who is not only a bouncer but also a first aider, immediately notices that Frank is lying there completely motionless and eerily still. Sinkevicius, on the other hand, has a completely bloodstained face, but still moves his hand. So, the bouncer takes care of McGarahan and immediately starts first aid measures: he puts him in a stable lateral position and does mouth-to-mouth resuscitation. His hands shake as he makes the necessary compressions and waits to see if the man starts breathing on his own again. But the chest remains still.

In fact, the banker is so badly injured that he falls into a coma - one from which he will never wake up. He is taken by rescue workers to Addenbrooke's Hospital in Cambridge. But the head injuries are too severe. Due to brain haemorrhages, he dies the next day - the day he was supposed to attend his niece's baptism. He pays for his civil courage with his life.

On Sunday morning, the priest of the Roman Catholic Church in Norwich, who was supposed to hold Thea's baptism, also receives a phone call. The family informs the surprised priest that the baptism planned for 11 am has been cancelled and a funeral is to be planned instead.

The Good Samaritan

On September 30, two days after the fatal fight, the Cowles brothers turn themselves in. Tom (22), a builder, and his 21-year-old brother Ben, who works as a plumber, admit that they were both there during the attack. However, they admit that they only reacted when they were called "cowards". The men, however, would have attacked them first and the Norwich brothers would only have defended themselves.

Even without the camera surveillance and the testimony of the eye witnesses, the background of the two young men, who were still living with their father at the time, would already have been a cause for doubts. Like their victim, Frank McGarahan, the two men also come from humble backgrounds. But while Frank was always goal-oriented and made the best of his abilities, the Cowles brothers can look back on a past where violence is a recurring theme.

Especially fatal for Frank McGarahan: Both are experienced boxers. As teenagers, they learned boxing for two years at the Norwich Lads' Club and never missed a single training session. And they had great talent, as their coach at the time confirmed. So, Tom was named young club boxing talent of the year in 2000 and 2001, while Ben went on to win the title of Eastern Counties Champion in 2000. Unfortunately, Ben suffers a head injury in a fight, which causes him to suffer from recurring severe headaches. When he quits boxing because of this, his brother also quits out of loyalty. The two are connected by a very close bond.

But while strict discipline always prevailed in the boxing club and it was clear that one should refrain from inferior persons or not attack them at all, the brothers begin to use their skills on the streets as well. In 2001, Tom receives a warning for an attack. Three years later, Ben is also reprimanded for a similar offence.

Their academic career at Norwich's Costessey High School is not very spectacular, and the two eventually choose craft professions. But the propensity to violence and also heavy drinking will continue to determine their lives, as a Facebook post from Tom shortly before the attack on September 28, 2008 shows. He posts his favourite line: "One went bang, two fell over." One struck, two fell to the ground.

The trial will start in early summer 2009, and in June the verdict will finally be delivered, which will cause a stir.

Based on the surveillance videos documenting the incidents in the early morning of September 28, 2008, the course of events can be easily reconstructed. The prosecutor points out that the "neutral" posture of the two McGarahans and Sean Ryan can be clearly seen when they cross over to the group of youths. They show no aggression whatsoever - the attack on them is therefore without any form of provocation. However, this is exactly what the Cowles brothers stated during the police interrogation. The footage shows that this is merely an act motivated by moral courage.

During the trial, several members of the McGarahan family also spoke out. Their statements make it clear how tragic the loss of 45-year-old Frank is for them all. Especially as he leaves his beloved wife Alison with his only three-month-old daughter fatherless. Both of his children will have to grow up without the care and attention of their father.

The lawyers of Ben and Tom Cowles, in turn, are trying to obtain a fair trial for their clients, because in their opinion the fairness towards the brothers has been severely jeopardised by the great media interest. According to Ben's lawyer, the media has stylised Frank McGarahan as a kind of hero who rushed to the rescue. In fact, by the time he and his companions arrived, the fight between the young people and Sinkevicius had already ended. The trio had provoked the young men and used strong expressions to antagonise them. In this respect, it was very questionable whether McGarahan had actually come as a saviour or not. In addition, the lawyer points out the good character of his client.

Tom's defence attorney also stresses that no weapons were used. The attack was neither an act of revenge nor was it intentional. And he calls his client a "great young man".

Their strategy is clear: they must do everything they can to convince the jury that their clients had no intention of killing in the attack or that they had no intention of seriously injuring their bodies.

The brothers finally plead guilty to both acts - the attack on Sinkevicius and the attack on Frank McGarahan. However, they plead not guilty to the charge of murder.

When Judge Saunders finally announces the verdict, many observers and the McGarahan family are shocked. The original charge of murder is dropped. 21-year-old Ben Cowles is sentenced to seven and a half years in prison for manslaughter, 22-year-old Tom even gets half a year less.

The 22-year-old carpenter Daniel Moy, who attacked Sean Ryan, will have to pay almost 60 euros in compensation as well as complete 100 hours of social service.

In the reasons for the verdict, the judge points out that he is aware of how difficult it must be for the victim's family in particular to understand the decision on manslaughter. In this respect, the verdict will inevitably be perceived as too lenient and criticised. However, he said that the verdict was reasonable, and that the penalty was set at this level by the law. The maximum penalty had been exhausted with good reason. In the end, the reasons for the verdict almost seem like an excuse to the trial observers.

Saunders is apparently aware of how difficult it is for the relatives of a killed victim to understand fine legal definitions of terms. Because for them, it doesn't matter what the murderer's intention was when he committed the crime. While the perpetrators will be released after a few years, the family of Frank McGarahan has received a life sentence.

In fact, Tony McGarahan, the victim's older brother, will subsequently describe the verdict as downright "shamefully low" and call for an urgent general review of the legislation on homicides of all kinds. For him, the verdict is a tragedy, leaving behind two small children who will never get to know their wonderful, brave father.

CHAPTER SIXTEEN:

A simple, white pocket watch

(by Amrei Baumgartl / „Darf's ein bisserl Mord sein?")

Charles Walton is a loner, yet he is respected and appreciated in Lower Quinton, in the Stratford-on-Avon district. He spent his entire life in the small town where he was born on May 12, 1870, the son of Charles and Emma Walton. He worked as a farmhand and was hired on the surrounding farms for casual work. However, his rheumatism was becoming increasingly troublesome, so he ended up leaning on a stick to assist with his walking. In his youth, Walton is considered an exceptionally good horse trainer, and the animals follow him at the slightest hint. In general, he has a better relationship with animals than he did with people, only with one friend, George Higgins, he maintains closer contact over the years.

Yet Charles Walton is not a monster, for when his sister, who lives in Stratford, dies, he takes in his three-year-old niece Edith Isabel without much ado in his house - although her father is still alive. When she is old enough, she takes over the housework for the older, disabled man. In return, Edith receives a small wage from him as well as free board and lodging. Even when she gets a job as a printing assistant at the Royal Society of Arts during the Second World War, which moved its headquarters to Quinton during the war, she continues to live with her uncle.

The mysterious events, whose centre will be around the 75-year-old Charles Walton, take place in the last months of the Second World War in 1945. More precisely, on Valentine's Day. On February 14th, the elderly man leaves his house with a pitchfork and a hoe, a sickle-shaped tool that can be used in many ways in woodwork and yard work. Since he has no intention of buying anything, he leaves his wallet at home. He sets off for Hillground, where on that day he is to trim hedges for his current employer, Alfred Potter, the tenant of "The Firs " estate. Between 9 and 9:30 eyewitnesses see him crossing the cemetery.

A simple, white pocket watch

Around 6:00 p.m., Edith comes home from work. She finds the house empty, which is highly unusual, because her uncle usually returns from work around 4pm at the latest. So, Edith immediately sets off in search of him; the young woman asks the neighbour Harry Beasley for help.

Together they first visit the farm of Alfred Potter, Walton's current employer, to ask him if he knows where the elderly man is. Potter claims to have seen the worker cutting hedges in Hillground earlier in the day but has not spoken to him. Potter joins Edith and Beasley and together the three of them go to the property in question in Hillground. But they did not expect what awaits them there.

In fact, Walton is still at the hedges. But the old man is dead. Killed in an incredibly brutal way.

It is almost as if the culprit wanted to make some kind of mark with this murder. Because Walton was first hit on the head by his attacker, then had his neck slit with his own scythe. But that's not all: with a massive blow of the pitchfork, his body was literally nailed to the ground, the tines driven through his neck into the earth.

Through Edith's shocked screams, a neighbour from the village, Harry Peachey, who is walking along the other side of the hedge, becomes aware of the trio. Beasley asks the walker to alert the police immediately. He then takes

Edith home and tells Alfred Potter to wait for the police at the scene of the crime.

The first officer arrives at the scene around seven o'clock in the evening, a little later other colleagues appear. The forensic expert James M. is only in Hillground at half past eleven at night, and at half past one at night Walton's body is finally taken away.

The same evening, the Detective Inspector of the region, Tombs, visits Alfred Potter, the tenant of the estate "The Firs", to which the property in Hillground also belongs. He says that he has employed Walton for the past nine months on a regular basis, and that the two had known each other for five years prior. The hedges at Hillground would have been the last work agreed for the time being. Potter went on to say that he had been out with another farmer that morning and had seen Walton at work on his way home.

The local police are groping in the dark. They suspect, as stated in a statement by the lead investigator in Warwickshire on February 15, that either a madman committed the crime or an Italian prisoner of war from a nearby internment camp. Only the time of death can be narrowed down relatively clearly by the forensic scientist. The murder must have taken place between one and two o'clock in the afternoon, and a pocket watch was also

A simple, white pocket watch

stolen from the dead man. This simple, white metal pocket watch with a snap-lock on the back, a dial of white enamel and the text "Edgar Jones, Stratford-on-Avon" is the only valuable object that Charles Walton always carried with him. It is the subject of an intensive manhunt, in the hope of catching the culprit along with it.

As early as February 16, Chief Inspector Robert Honey Fabian, who became one of the first and best-known crime writers after his retirement, and his colleague Detective Albert Webb, arrive from London as supporting investigators. They are followed shortly afterwards by Sergeant Saunders, who speaks fluent Italian, and who is to take over the interrogations of the Italian prisoners of war.

The main suspect, however, is Alfred Potter, so a police officer is assigned to follow him and his wife. Saunders starts investigating at the Long Marston internment camp. The prisoners there enjoy relatively great freedom of movement, so some of them went to Stratford on the afternoon of the day of the murder to see a play, while others went to see a film screening. However, Saunders cannot identify a suspect here.

The autopsy by the forensic scientist Professor Webster shows that Walton's windpipe was cut. He also finds injuries to the head and some broken ribs on the rib cage.

Walton also has clearly visible defensive injuries, such as bruises on his back, right forearm, and right hand. According to Webster, everything points to the pitchfork and the scythe as the weapons of choice. The perpetrator inflicted the head injuries on Walton by hitting him on the head with his own walking stick. The stick was found about three metres from the body, with blood and hair still stuck to it. The forensic scientist noted something else unusual: the dead man's shirt was torn open, his waistband unbuttoned, and his fly unbuttoned. However, Webster's report does not mention a cross carved on Walton's chest, which appears repeatedly in other records.

On February 17, Alfred Potter is again questioned by the police, this time about the employment relationship of Charles Walton. Among other things, Potter expresses the suspicion that Walton cheated him several times with regard to the number of hours actually worked, i.e. he declared more hours than he did. The last time Potter had paid the 75-year-old was on February 10th, four days before the murder. When he saw him working in the field at a distance on the day of the murder, he had actually wanted to go to Charles, but a calf had been trapped in a ditch and needed help. For this reason, Potter went straight home again afterwards. Based on the time Potter claims to have seen Walton and the remaining piece of hedge at the time, a period of death can be assumed - this in turn coincides with the result of the autopsy.

When the police return to Alfred Potter's farm on February 20 to secure potentially usable evidence, Potter comes up with a surprising explanation. Suddenly, it is said that he touched the hoe and almost certainly the pitchfork when he found the body. Therefore, it is possible that his fingerprints could be discovered. Potter claims that the neighbour Harry Beasley instructed him to check whether Charles Walton was really dead. For the investigators, the question now is whether Potter wants to dispel suspicions in advance? So far, he had never said a word about it.

The suspect insists that the murder was "the work of one of the fascists from the (prisoner) camp". The situation becomes increasingly acute, but then another policeman appears in the yard and reports surprising things: The military has just arrested one of the Italian prisoners, who had blood on his clothes. Suddenly, the Potter couple appears to be liberated. The woman even breaks out into hysterical laughter.

Was this information only a test of the police, who wanted to know how the Potters would react? In any case, the investigation against the Italian quickly fizzles out.

Alfred Potter has been suspected for a long time and numerous points speak against him: Potter was used to slaughtering animals and investigations revealed that the calf, which allegedly needed Potter's help, had already drowned the day before. Regarding the alleged alibis, inconsistencies also arise, they partly contradict each other during the plot and in the timing. After several inquiries, Potter also revised his initially concrete statement that he had seen Charles Walton in the fields by the hedge at noon. In the end, all that is said is that he saw a person standing there. Furthermore, Potter explains his fingerprints on the murder weapons with the fact that Beasley had asked him to check whether Walton was still alive. But Beasley claims that he didn't ask for any such thing. And finally, with regard to payroll payments in general, information is emerging that has an impact on Potter's reputation. In fact, he appears to be embezzling funds; as a manager, he is asking the owner for higher salaries than those he actually pays.

However, despite all these contradictions, the police are unable to find any compelling evidence to prove that Potter is the murderer. Moreover, there is no motive for the crime. No "plausible reason" can be found that points to Potter being the killer. Since he can provide alibis for the period of the crime from some employees and neighbours who saw him or whom he allegedly helped, the police finally drop the investigation against him.

In return, the law enforcement officers also find strange things in Charles Walton's supposedly so inconspicuous life - more precisely in his finances. According to Edith, her uncle never borrowed or lent money. In 1930 he had deposited over 227 pounds with the Midland Bank (today over 17,000 euros), but this sum shrank to just over 11 pounds in 1939 (about 800 euros). It is noteworthy, however, that Walton only withdrew smaller amounts over the years, at most 10 pounds. How can this be explained? Where did all this money go?

This is the reason for emerging speculation that Potter may have borrowed money. When the 75-year-old finally demanded repayment, Potter had not been able to pay and therefore got rid of the annoying creditor. But there is no evidence of this.

Charles Walton's best friend, George Higgins, 72 years old, is also a suspect. Higgins, who, like Charles, lives from field and farm work, is said to have worked in a barn not far from the crime scene on the day of the murder. It would have been easy for him to brutally murder his best friend and then return to his work. But there is no motive for the crime, and the older field worker is denied the necessary strength for the attack.

All in all, more than 500 people are interviewed during the investigation, children as well as elderly people. Even travellers who were passing through the small town at the time of the crime will be found and questioned. But all without success.

The more hopeless the police investigation becomes, the more desperate the search for explanations. So, more and more attention is paid to the history of the village. This leads to first suspicions that maybe supernatural powers were involved in this murder. One of the investigators draws inspiration for his research from the book *Old Customs and Superstitions in Shakespeare Land,* written by the local clergyman James Harvey Bloom in 1929 about the area around Stratford-on-Avon. Among other things, it mentions the murder of a 79-year-old woman named Ann Tennant, who was murdered in 1875 by a family friend who accused her of witchcraft. Relevant for the investigation in Walton's murder is above all the death of the alleged witch, who was executed in a similar way, having been impaled on the ground with a pitchfork.

Another story in this book makes the investigators pay attention: The author notes that in 1885 a little boy on his way home from field work is said to have seen a black dog for eight days in a row, on the ninth day the dog was even accompanied by a headless lady. On this very evening, the boy learns that his sister has died. The name of the child: Charles Walton.

However, it is unclear whether the boy is really the man who was later murdered. But the age could be right.

Black dogs are regarded in the region as harbingers of death and also in 1945 a dead black dog is said to have hung from a tree not far from where the body was found.

Because of his reclusive way of life, Charles Walton was also repeatedly accused of witchcraft. He had taken advantage of this during horse training. A witness also says that Charles Walton spoke the language of the birds and asked the birds not to eat the seeds scattered in his fields - with success.

Indeed, the region around Lower Quinton is the scene of many legends and stories about higher powers, magic, and sorcery. It is said that not far from where the body was found, an old stone circle can be found in a druid cemetery. Was the brutal murder of Charles Walton perhaps connected with the rituals of the Druids or followers of old cults? Could the old man have been a blood sacrifice?

When the adjoining building of Charles Walton's house is demolished in 1960, a worker makes a surprising discovery. He finds a shimmering object among the rubble: it is Walton's pocket watch, which disappeared in 1945. When it is opened, there is a piece of "witches' glass" inside. Witch glass, it was believed, reflects and/or absorbs all negative vibrations sent to the person wearing an object.

But that is not even the most amazing thing about the find. Much stranger is the fact that the police thoroughly searched the entire property immediately after the crime and that the watch seemed to have disappeared from the face of the earth. Could the killer have put it back over time? Or had it not been searched for as meticulously as the whole world had been led to believe? However, this clue in 1960 was the last in the still unsolved murder case of Charles Walton.

CHAPTER SEVENTEEN:

An immortal soul

Although there are icy temperatures on this January 18 and a very cold wind is blowing, Constable Kenneth G. does not notice. He is much too concentrated on the task at hand. His eyes are focused on the spongy ground in the small forest, his gaze searching every square inch. Not for the first time in recent days. The forest area is located northwest of the small Scottish town of Fauldhouse. The boggy ground gives way under every step. Finally, the Constable has worked his way up to the next drainage ditch. From a distance, what is sticking out of the muddy water may look like a broken branch. But when the Constable realises its true nature, he suddenly feels sick. His whole body feels hot and icy cold at the same time. Because what is down there is ... a hand with a forearm. The fingers are slightly curved, as if they were trying to grab something during their last moment of movement.

Kenneth G. closes his eyes trembling - now the body of Thomas McKendrick has finally been found.

The small Scottish town of Fauldhouse in the West Lothian region is in a state of shock at the turn of the year 2002 to 2003. The search for 21-year-old Thomas McKendrick has been feverishly going on for weeks. The young man has been missing since December 11, nobody had an idea where he could be. He is considered to be an extremely friendly person who is loved by everyone. He has no enemies, so it is unimaginable that he could have crossed anyone. Also, there is nothing known about possible problems or worries that might have burdened him so much that he might go into hiding or run away. Therefore, everyone is puzzling over what might have happened to Thomas. His worried parents have informed the police, who interviewed all his friends and acquaintances as part of their investigation. Among them was his friend, 22-year-old, Allan Menzies.

Menzies, whose parents Thomas and Linda are already divorced at this time, is considered a quiet young man who has few friends and likes to keep to himself. After school he works as security for a while. Allan and Thomas have known each other since they were both four years old. Even as teenagers and young adults they spend a lot of time together and become best friends over the years. Unfortunately, Allan can't give the investigators any clue where Thomas is or what might have happened to him.

So, the Fauldhouse police continue their tireless search. At the beginning of 2003, they are already sure that something terrible must have happened to Thomas. And on January 4 of the New Year, the vague, unpleasant suspicion finally turns into a terrible certainty: when the police comb through one of the small, wooded areas surrounding Fauldhouse again, they discover a bag. Full to the brim. Someone had obviously gone through great trouble to hide it in the undergrowth between leaves. Inside it, they find some clothes. Bloody! And they are the clothes Thomas was wearing the day he disappeared. This makes it clear: The 21-year-old did not run away, but this is clearly a violent crime. But where is the body?

Two days later, on January 6, Allan Menzies is again questioned by the police about the case. The police station is suspicious because Allan's home, which Thomas visited on December 11, is his last known whereabouts. The young man also asked the mother of the missing person if she had any idea how to remove bloodstains from clothes. During this interrogation, Menzies reaffirms that he does not know where his friend might be. The last time he saw him was on December 11. However, he assumes that

Thomas is still alive because he has spoken to him twice since then.

Doesn't Allan know at this time that Thomas' bloody clothes have been found? The policemen, at any rate, do not hesitate a moment longer and take their measures. They drive to the Menzies' house on Langrigg Avenue. In order to prevent the most important witness in this case from making evidence disappear, the house is cleared immediately and then sealed for the time being. The residents must leave the house and can only gather their most important belongings under the watchful eye of the police.

Then a tense calm will return. It's a bit like the calm before the storm, as everyone waits for the police to finally take a closer look at the Menzies' house. Is this really where clues about Thomas' whereabouts are waiting, or are Allan's shenanigans perhaps just an attempt by a young man to cover up something else? What will come to light during the investigation will change the lives of the people in the small Scottish town of Fauldhouse forever. But that's not all: in the future, the inhabitants of the whole of Great Britain will ask themselves where the boundaries between reality and fiction lie and whether the two may overlap.

From now on, events in the town take a tumultuous turn. For on January 9, Mr Menzies is shocked to discover that his son has tried to take his own life via overdose. Luckily, he finds him in the shared temporary accommodation just in time for the doctors to save him. But instead of being grateful, Allan later calls his father from the hospital and angrily accuses him of not letting him die.

The attempted suicide only alarms the investigators in the McKendrick murder case even more: On January 10 and 11, intensive house searches are carried out at the Menzies' homes, focusing primarily on the rooms Allan occupies. What the police find there deeply disturbs them. They are mainly looking at videos and books; they're all about vampires! In addition to a copy of the film "Queen of the Damned", they discover a book from the series "Chronicle of the Vampires" by the writer Anne Rice, which attracts their attention, because there are handwritten comments and notes in the margin for numerous passages, with a large number of spelling mistakes. On one of the pages he neatly noted: "Blood is life, I drank the blood and it shall be mine, for I have seen the horror."

According to the results of these searches, there can only be one decision: Police arrest Allan Menzies on January 20, 2003 - although no body has yet been found. After all, his behaviour is more than just peculiar. But what now follows will later be described as grotesque and extremely disturbing by the two policemen who bring the young man to the examining magistrate for a summons on January 22. It almost seems as if Menzies is really happy to finally be able to talk openly to someone. The 22-year-old appears relaxed and speaks to the two men while driving. He asks the policemen what they think will happen for him. Menzies thinks aloud that he will probably get 20 to 25 years for killing "him" with a hammer and his Bowie knife. "But," he continues in the interview, "I got his soul." And then Menzies adds: "I drank his blood and ate a bite of his head. There was blood everywhere and I buried him in the woods."

Why he is talking about everything now, nobody really knows. Maybe Allan feels convicted. But there it is, a confession! And Menzies just confesses as if he was meeting up with some good friends for a cosy tea and talking about the weather. And he's just now reporting that he killed his best friend and buried him in the ground! But that's not all - there's also talk of cannibalism! For blood and a soul?

But Menzies isn't finished with his cosy chat yet. Later on, during the trial, the police officers will state that the young man then openly thought that he would manage to get into the psychiatric ward of Carstairs State Hospital if he pleaded guilty. Menzies then remains there in the psychiatric ward for a full five months until the trial begins. Later he says was very disappointed that there were no other vampires there.

But first, the court of inquiry orders on January 22 that Allan Menzies be sent to Saughton prison near Edinburgh. From there he sends letters to himself - home. Letters in which he announces that he will kill again. The lines are signed with the word "vampire", written in his own blood. Because the staff fear that he might attempt suicide, he is later transferred to Carstairs for the time being.

Still, in January 2003, the horribly mutilated body of Thomas Kendrick is finally found in a forest area near Fauldhouse. The findings of the forensic medicine are shocking and prove a level of brutality that is hardly imaginable. It is thought that Allan Menzies hit his best, long-time friend over ten times on the head with a hammer, crushing his skull. But that's not all: He also stabbed him with a knife in a blood frenzy. The blade penetrated his head, face, and body a total of 42 times. There are four puncture marks in McKendrick's neck alone, at least one on his hip. One stab also goes right through his throat up to the brain! It's an almost unbearable sight, even for the most hard-boiled coroners.

And then, as life slowly seeped out of Thomas, his best friend must have caught the warm, viscous, dark red liquid in a container. Full of greed to savour the taste, which is similar to copper.

After the confession, the murder weapons are also finally found in the moor, but not at the place where the body was deposited. Obviously, the killer separated all incriminating clues and hid them in different places: the bloodstained clothes in a bag, the body in a drainage ditch, the weapons in another hiding place. In doing so, he always made sure to place them at the greatest possible distance. He apparently proceeded in a very purposeful and thoughtful manner, not like someone who is panic-stricken after an act of passion.

The trial of the self-proclaimed Fauldhouse vampire, which will be heard by the High Court in Edinburgh from October 8, 2003 onwards, under the presidency of Judge Roderick MacDonald, is attracting widespread public interest. And what will emerge from the investigation will indeed be so spectacular and eccentric that most people cannot even begin to comprehend it. The wildest fantasies will even be surpassed in the end, because in the coming days of the trial one will dive deep into the confused world of thoughts of the young defendant.

Allan Menzies is downright obsessed by the thought of the existence of vampires, supernatural beings who feed on the blood of their victims and can thus live for all eternity.

An immortal soul

Without aging, without dying. Powerful beings who are not bound by earthly constraints. He is particularly fond of the book series "Chronicle of the Vampires" by the writer Anne Rice, but above all the film adaptation with the title "Queen of the Damned". During the search, the police found a worn-out copy of this film in Menzies' room. It turns out that it was already the second video cassette, because it ran again and again. Allan saw the film 100 times, at least three times a day, in the month before December 11. He immersed himself deeply into the world of the plot, whose main character is the powerful vampire queen Akasha (in the film played by the late singer Aaliyah). Menzies is so caught up in his thoughts that he finally believes that this Akasha visits him at his home and has conversations with him. Conversations, at the end of which the two finally make a deal: Akasha will reward him in the next life for killing people in this one. His reward: He shall receive an immortal vampire soul.

Does the thought already germinate in him now of killing his only good friend Thomas and drinking his blood and eating a piece of his flesh? Was this cruel murder deliberate?

Or was it more like Menzies - or Leon, as he calls himself from now on in reference to one of the film characters - wants the court to believe it? He claims that the murder was committed in the heat of passion. For Thomas had made the terrible mistake of insulting the vampire figure Akasha and making fun of her. And at that moment, Menzies only wanted to punish him. He hit his buddy on the head full of rage and stabbed him several times.

Finally, Menzies explained to the court that he had become a vampire and from that moment on immortal. And at the same time, the desire had grown in him to go out into the world and kill people.

Does Menzies himself realise how strange and abstruse this description of his thoughts and feelings sounds? For he explains that at the moment of the attack he must have been suffering from an episode of paranoid schizophrenia, which is why he lost control of his mind. As if to substantiate this, he speaks of hearing voices, too. Voices whispering to him that Thomas, together with another friend named Stuart, were planning a murder plot against him.

What effect did this version of the story have on the two policemen who brought Allan to the Saughton Court of Inquiry on January 22? On that trip, Allan had confessed to the murder and was already thinking about the possible sentence and even about his defence strategy. Both police officers are also present at this trial before the High Court.

And they emphasise in their statements that the young killer did not appear particularly agitated or confused. On the contrary, he appeared to them very thoughtful and clear. Could the alleged insanity that clouded Allan's mind be simply a perfidious strategy to escape a prison sentence?

Because, obviously, Allan stops at nothing to improve his own position. At the trial he will also testify that he had accomplices in his crime. Allegedly his own father, Thomas Menzies, who he claims disposed of the victim's body. Also, that he was assisted by his friend Stuart. On the Monday after the crime, the two men brought the body in a dumpster in the wooded area of Fauldhouse Moor around 2 a.m. and dumped it in the drainage ditch. Trustfully, Allan then also gives assurances that he had said nothing until that moment, so as not to harm his father.

His shocked reaction, however, is clear. Thomas Menzies knows nothing about a dumpster or a pond.

It is precisely the clarification of the guiltiness that will become an essential point in the following trial. The psychiatric expert for the defendant supports Menzies' statement that he suffers from paranoid schizophrenia and can therefore only be guilty to a lesser degree. However, three other experts clearly rule out this diagnosis and certify that the young man suffers rather from an "antisocial personality disorder". Characteristics of this include a lack of remorse, repeated lying, the use of aliases, impulsiveness and aggressiveness, the inability to pursue permanent employment, and the inability to comply with laws and social norms. A strong imagination, yes. But insanity? No.

Menzie's prehistory, which is also discussed, shows that violence and sadism are part of his character, because he stabbed a classmate in the eye with a knife in 1996 and had to spend three years in a psychiatric hospital in Glasgow. His mother, Linda Menzies (49), also describes him as mentally impaired. Allan had stayed in his darkened room for days as a child and showed signs of hospitalism. Changes could cause panic attacks. Already at an early age he had tried to hurt himself and commit suicide with pills.

Finally, the overall picture of the statements points to an extremely difficult, violent personality of the accused - but does he actually show signs of a massive mental illness that renders him incapable of guilt?

In conclusion, the "Vampire of Scotland" pleads guilty - but only guilty of murder in the heat of passion with reduced capacity for guilt.

The judge's stance is clear and unambiguous: he does not acknowledge any guilt-mitigating circumstances whatsoever but sees Menzies simply as an "evil and dangerous psychopath" who must be locked away. Allan

Menzies is finally sentenced to at least 18 years in prison before he can file a pardon petition.

After the trial, Menzies' lawyer will emphasise that this sentence is evidence of how society stigmatises mental illness. However, the murdered man's sister, Sandra-Mary (23), is certain: "He got what he deserved. I firmly believe he is not mentally ill; it was just acting."

On November 15, 2004, Allan Menzies is found dead. He hung himself with his sheet on a metal grille outside the window of his solitary cell in Shotts Prison, Glasgow. A suicide note is not found. What motivated Allan Menzies to take this step? Belief in an afterlife as an immortal vampire? Remorse for what he did? Or was this possibly another suicide attempt by a mentally ill person, but this time no one came to the rescue in time?

CHAPTER EIGHTEEN:

Stumbling block for the wrong person

As he is about to leave the courthouse in September 2009, the horde of journalists is already waiting for him. Suddenly, a thunderstorm of flashlights sets in and camera headlights illuminate him so much that the man is almost blinded. Microphones are held in front of the Chief Inspector's face from everywhere, all eagerly awaiting his statement. After all, he was the one who for nine years believed that the culprit would be apprehended. What was his opinion about the trial? What did he think about the defendant? Brent Hyatt gathers a moment before he speaks. But then he replies with disarming honesty: "He has proven to be a highly arrogant, compulsive, skilled liar, driven by a desire to make money." What he does not add, however: And who really went over dead bodies to achieve his goal.

When Michael Lanitis acquires the building complex in Kensal Rise, in north-west London, in 1978, he has big plans for it. He has some apartments built in and runs a wholesale business for food, beer, and wine. The combination of eating/shopping and living is a very innovative project for that time. One of the Lanitis employees at the time was his brother-in-law, Charalambos Christodoulides, a quiet, friendly man who is addressed only as "Bambi". His elongated face with slightly clouded eyes, which are hidden behind large glasses, shows his intelligence. Originally, Christodoulides studied economics, but he prefers to work for Lanitis. This employment relationship only ends when he is injured by a barrel accident, leaving him disabled. Since then, the Cypriot has led a quiet, secluded life - only interrupted by trips to the city, during which he likes to appear like a distinguished gentleman, wearing noble, tailor-made suits, visiting small restaurants and studying the results of the horse races. After all, his little personal luxury is to bet a few pounds on fast thoroughbreds at the bookmaker every now and then.

In 1993, Lanitis closes the department store for good and moves away with his family. Christodoulides, who does not want to move, is given the task of looking after the building complex. Occasionally, he receives visits from his relatives who help him clean up his apartment, but he also goes to them every Sunday to eat with them.

Nevertheless, on Sunday, March 12, 2000, the family is concerned about the 57-year-old Christodoulides, when he does not join them for dinner. It is not until the following Thursday, March 16, that they finally become restless and contact the police.

The police cannot find any traces of a break-in in the department store where Christodoulides lived. During the search, they find Christodoulides' wallet and glasses, his bus ticket, and some traces of blood. The most recent newspaper in his apartment, which the police find, is dated March 10. His bus ticket, with which he went to the bookmaker, expired on March 9, and has not been renewed. Nor did he pick up his winnings at the betting shop. At first, the police suspect amnesia, but the worried family is not satisfied with this explanation and demands further investigations be made.

Nine days later, on Saturday March 25, when the department store is searched again, the officers take a much more meticulous approach - and make a real discovery!

This time the search is extended to the garage area integrated into the department store, which also contains a workshop pit. When the police officers shine their lights briefly into the dark pit, their breath stops. There is something down there! Only sheets and garbage bags can be seen from above. The bundle at the bottom of the pit, however, does not bode well. As the policemen descend and carefully remove the cover, the first thing that strikes them is a pervasive chemical smell. Paint remover! Then they uncover the body.

Two days later, the deceased can finally be identified: It is indeed the 57-year-old Christodoulides. And there are signs that someone tortured and tormented him before his death. Traces of blood suggest that the man was previously tied to a chair and that he wore a hood during the maltreatment. Strangulation marks on his neck further indicate that he was eventually strangled.

Everyone is shocked and distraught as Charalambos Christodoulides was described by his relatives as friendly, gentle, and reserved. Hence his nickname "Bambi". Why did such a person have to die such a brutal death? The policemen are also at a loss as to why his murderers made such an enormous effort to make the body unrecognizable. Only the time of death can be determined more precisely: The murder must have happened after the visit to the betting shop. Traces on site also indicate that the disabled man was attacked in front of the building and then dragged inside. Although the perpetrators have so meticulously tried to make the body unrecognizable, they have made no attempt to cover their own tracks, so that the investigators can secure both DNA and fingerprints.

As the investigators continue their investigation, a name suddenly crops up that no one would have expected: Thanos Papalexis.

In London, at the turn of the millennium, Thanos Papalexis is an established member of society. The 37-year-old son of a Greek shipping magnate, a handsome dark-haired man with a square chin that gives his face a particularly energetic expression, joined the family business after graduating from university and then energetically diversified it. He developed it away from shipping and oil trading and towards real estate trading. His empire includes several companies in the real estate investment and hospitality sectors. He became known through real estate leasing, among other things, with a particular focus on Florida, USA. He became legendary through a very special deal: When a high-rise complex in West Palm Beach was damaged in a hurricane, he conducted purchase negotiations with each of the 119 owners. The young entrepreneur's extreme tenacity and ambition earned him great respect in the industry, even when the deal went bust.

In his deals, Papalexis often acts as a "locust" - he buys a cheap old property, giving the impression that he wants to revitalise and develop it. In fact, however, he does everything he can to sell the buildings again as quickly as possible - at a profit, of course. He only pays the seller when he receives the amount from the subsequent sale, which makes such a deal for Papalexis both cost-neutral and highly profitable. The earnings, in turn, are used to finance other, parallel projects, in which he unfortunately often has no luck, or to enable his expensive lifestyle.

Papalexis enjoys the life of a playboy and millionaire to the fullest - especially during his time in the US. He wears expensive suits, furnishes his business premises and apartments in the USA with golden thrones. Among other things, this involves the beach villa of murdered fashion guru Gianni Versace in Florida, the Casa Casuarina. You see him driving around in a Bentley or Lamborghini. But also, lavish parties are exactly his style. He especially likes to surround himself with important personalities and celebrities like Paris Hilton and designer Valentino, or organises fundraising events for Hillary Clinton, at which her husband, ex-president Bill Clinton, is also present.

His reputation as a playboy is cemented by his numerous changing female acquaintances, among whom are also high-class prostitutes and film stars of the porn scene. After all, rumour has it that the ambitious Greek-born businessman and real estate developer is also interested in deviant sexual practices.

The fact is, however, that Papalexis is getting more and more into financial trouble due to his expensive lifestyle and inappropriate behaviour in shady business matters. Increasingly, he is manoeuvring himself into social extinction. For example, he receives countless fraud reports because his project for a deluxe residential club in Florida turns out to be a blip in the radar. The promised amenities such as private jets and expensive rental cars are not kept. The property developer does not pay the rent for the Versace Villa and his checks bounce immediately.

In spring 2000, Papalexis is in London, where once again one of his "locust deals" is up for interim financing. This time the property of choice is the old, abandoned department store in Kensal Rise, where the modest Christodoulides lives. A year earlier, Michael Lanitis decided to sell the property. Once again, the 37-year-old Papalexis is in an extreme financial jam, because another risky real estate deal from 1999 is about to fail. The cheap illegal craftsmen are too inexperienced and deliver poor work right from the start. The creditors are standing Papalexis on his feet and he urgently needs money. When Lanitis signals that Papalexis can buy the department store in Kensal Rise for 2.000.000 pounds, Papalexis takes direct action. Lanitis has no idea that the millionaire has no intention of renovating or rebuilding the property. He is only aiming for his own profit.

However, Christodoulides now comes into play, which becomes a stumbling block. Despite his previous assurances to Lanitis that he would move out of his apartment if necessary, he now suddenly refuses. Papalexis is sitting on hot coals - every week that Christodoulides stays in the apartment he can't resell the complex. In plain language: the refusal costs Papalexis a whopping 60,000 pounds a week. When police investigators become aware of this fact, they are immediately alarmed. This is a clear motive!

But they are too late, the millionaire has already fled to the USA. Due to the failed real estate deal he suddenly finds himself in the chalk with 8 million pounds and his creditors in London are extremely displeased. So, he unexpectedly eludes the police. Nevertheless, the investigators in England will stay on him for the next few years and do everything they can to solve the murder case. In the following nine months, they discover further DNA traces and fingerprints of other people in the department store - two other men must have been present here as well. This is a setback for the investigators, as the real estate agent is no longer the only suspect. But the policemen continue to investigate.

Meanwhile, Papalexis is in the USA, enjoying life to the fullest. He spends thousands of dollars on orgies with his changing playmates, whom he also likes to give breast implants. However, even his new business partners increasingly stumble upon the peculiarities of his special character. It seems as if Papalexis only accepts his own rules in his life.

Back in the UK, two men are arrested without much fuss in March 2008: the illegal immigrants from Albania Ylli Xhelo and Robert Baxhija. The reason for the arrest is actually only marijuana possession, but during the routine check with the database a small sensation occurs. The two craftsmen are clearly the men whose traces were also found in the department store. And again, the trace points to Papalexis, because the men were employees of the failed building project from 1999! On March 15, 2008 Xhelo and Baxhija are accused of the murder of Christodoulides. The prosecution fails, however, because they can plausibly explain that they did not commit the murder; they would only have cleaned up the crime scene and removed the body. The murderer was Papalexis. He had forced them at gunpoint to remove the traces of the crime. Once again, the millionaire comes into the focus of the investigation!

Nevertheless, Chief Inspector Brent Hyatt, who is responsible for the murder case, cannot strike directly - Papalexis is in the Bahamas at this time. Only on November 7, 2008, the bon vivant is arrested by US marshals in Florida while he is having dinner with a girlfriend.

For Hyatt, it is a stroke of luck when an important witness finally contacts him. This last "piece of the puzzle" is former hardcore porn star Rebecca DeFalco, who also worked as a luxury prostitute. She and Papalexis met during her time as a luxury escort. Their meetings were quite special, because the millionaire enjoyed watching her having sex with other men or indulging in sadomasochistic preferences with her. But much more important: Papalexis confessed the murder of Christodoulides to DeFalco! During a joint argument he explains: "Yes, I once strangled a man. He caused me problems." He then describes the crime in detail, mentioning the Kilburn department store and the failed deal.

The tabloids jump at the trial of millionaire and playboy Thanos Papalexis. It begins in June 2009 at the Old Bailey in London. The judge is Jeremy Roberts. In addition to the results of the police investigation, the testimony of Rebecca DeFalco is of great importance. Especially since the e-mail contact she has with Papalexis shortly before his arrest, which is read by prosecutor Laidlaw, throws a significant light on his character. When DeFalco writes to the millionaire that she is suffering from cancer, only a very short answer comes back from him: "Bon Voyage!".

During the trial, Papalexis is described as a "classic psychopath" who seeks satisfaction through criminal, sexual and aggressive impulses and is completely out of control here. He sees himself as being above the law, as a post from him on a sadomasochist website impressively underlines. In it he describes himself as "King of his own kingdom and all others shall be at his will".

Due to his inexperience, according to the defence, the defendant suffered heavy financial losses in 2000, which put him in a dangerous situation. Therefore, Papalexis desperately searched for a way out.

The real estate developer denies the murder of Christodoulides until the very end, but in his reasoning for the judgement, Judge Roberts points out that he was undoubtedly the one who gave the instructions and is therefore mainly responsible for the crime. The reason for the execution was simply greed and financial profit. For the judge, there is only one description for a person like Papalexis: he was a "completely amoral person".

The sentence is at least 20 years in prison.

Papalexis' accomplices, the Albanians Baxhija and Xhelo, who were also accused of murder, get off lightly at this trial. However, in a retrial on February 15 2010, they will also be found guilty of murder and will both receive a life sentence.

For Christodoulides' sister Anna it is inconceivable that Charalambos' life was extinguished because of the personal greed of a millionaire. Icy and calculating. In her written testimony in court she wrote: "I firmly believe that he is a kind of devil..."

But it also shows how desperately the relatives of the handicapped caretaker are trying to find some kind of sense for the torture and murder of this completely harmless man. Everything seems crooked and twisted. Why torture Christodoulides when he was supposed to be eliminated anyway? Or did Papalexis initially only plan to only intimidate the man who was in the way of his plans by torturing him? Was it perhaps simply a form of frustration because a person at the emotional level of a "spoiled child" did not get his way? And did he choose the means of strangulation for this purpose, but - possibly due to a kind of bloodlust - could not stop in time?

Probably the question why the victim, the man with roots on the sunny Mediterranean island of Cyprus, had to suffer in his last hours, will never be answered. Possibly he would have let himself be persuaded to move out by a severance package. But nothing was further from Papalexis' mind than to give away some of his profit. What remains is the memory of a friendly, reserved person, whom everyone called Bambi because of his dark eyes. A man whose only crime was to meet the wrong people in the wrong place at the wrong time.

CHAPTER NINETEEN:

Fatal lies

For Mary Sedotti, December 5 will be a day that will last forever, a day when she will think of her daughter Teresa over and over again. How would she look today? Would she have had a happy family? With many children? The mother with the short grey hair and sad eyes often remembers "her girl" Teresa, whom she describes as a shy but happy young woman. Photos of Teresa confirm this impression. What we see is a rather stocky, friendly-looking young woman with a 70s outer wave, smiling cautiously into the camera. A smile that will only be seen in photos after December 5, 1979.

Teresa Elena De Simone was born on June 24, 1957. The reserved young woman from Southampton stands on her own feet at the age of 22. She works full-time for the energy company Southern Gas. However, in order to be able to afford her first own car, a Ford Escort, and to make new contacts, she takes up a job as a barmaid in a pub at the beginning of November 1979 to work nights.

The "Tom Tackle" is centrally located, only 50 meters away from the police station and court buildings of Southampton. It is also only a short walk to the Central Station.

Teresa's shift ends on December 4 at around 11 pm; Teresa's friend Savage is already waiting to take her along. The two have decided to celebrate the birthday of another mutual friend Jenni in a disco. Together they go there with only one car. Shortly after midnight, Savage brings her friend back to the "Tom Tackle" where they arrive at the parking lot. The two friends stay in Savage's car for a while and talk, then De Simone says goodbye, gets out, and goes to her escort. Savage drives away. This is the last time she sees her friend alive.

The next morning, Teresa's mother finds out that her daughter did not come home that night. She asks her husband Michael, Teresa's stepfather, to go and see what's going on. He drives to the pub and sees the escort standing in the parking lot and turns back. He probably assumes that Teresa is staying with someone.

Shortly after 10 o'clock, Anthony P., the operator of the "Tom Tackle", comes to the pub. He expects a delivery of goods. Because Teresa's car is in the way, he wants to move it a little. As he stands directly in front of it and can look into the inside of the car, his breath stops. On the back seat lies a lifeless, half-naked body. It is Teresa. When Anthony can think clearly again, he immediately alarms the police.

The detectives come immediately and begin their investigation. De Simone was apparently brutally raped and then strangled. The perfidy: It looks like the murderer used his own necklace with the crucifix pendant for it! A circumstance that will later earn him the nickname "Crucifix Killer".

Around 11:45 a.m., the pathologist appears and examines the corpse, which lies on the back seat with spread legs. The left breast is exposed, the lower body is naked from the waist down. On one leg there are still remnants of her pantyhose, which has been pulled down to the ankle. The remaining part of the pantyhose as well as the underwear are in the foot area.

White, slimy foam in the dead woman's mouth proves that strangulation was indeed the cause of death. Scrape marks indicate the chain; it has disappeared - and will never be found. Also, the rest of the jewellery and car keys; Teresa's handbag and other personal belongings were left behind in the immediate vicinity. However, everyone involved is certain that this was not a robbery, but a brutal rape, after which the victim was strangled. Teresa's genitals show severe injuries and sperm is found in the vaginal canal. Due to the amount of sperm, the time of the crime can be narrowed down quite precisely: between 1am and 2am in the early morning of December 5.

Did the killer observe the two women and take action when Teresa was alone? Or was he possibly already sitting in her escort and waiting for her?

Based on the samples that the forensic experts take vaginally, anally, orally, as well as from the dead women's clothes and from the car, it later turns out that the killer must have blood type A or AB.

The following is one of the largest investigation campaigns of the British police, which will extend over a total of three years. During the first 12 months, about 30,000 people will be interviewed, 2,500 statements will be taken and 500 people who were near the "Tom Tackle" during the night will be checked. About 300 people will be classified as suspects.

Interestingly, the police also receive several anonymous messages. Still, in December, two letters are received, postmarked December 12 and 27, from Southampton. The investigators will remain silent about the contents for a long time, only in the court case will they state that the author gave hints about the whereabouts of the perpetrator

- all of them which proved to be false. The case is therefore dismissed as a silly joke.

Nine months later, the Southampton police receive two anonymous calls. The caller accuses himself of the murder of Teresa De Simone! He seems unusually tense and leaves the impression that he needs help and advice. Nevertheless, the police do not follow up on these clues.

At the same time, Sean Hodgson from Tow Law in County Durham is also in custody for another crime. Hodgson comes from an extended family and is sent to a home at the age of 11. At the time, his name is still Robert Graham, but he eventually changes it to Sean Hodgson, perhaps to distinguish himself from the family who did not prevent him from being placed in the home. He stands out early on for minor offences - most of them involving dishonesty and deception, although he seems to have a weakness for motor vehicles. Nevertheless, Hodgson is already a person with psychological abnormalities and problems. He is also prone to self-harming. In 1978, he is even in a clinic due to his several problems with overdosing on medication. He was diagnosed with a severe personality disorder and was found to be a "compulsive liar". Apparently, he is driven by an extremely strong craving for recognition and the urge to be the centre of attention.

On December 6, 1979, Southampton police arrested him for vehicle theft - only two days after he arrived in the city. The following day he gives the police a tip-off about a suspect in the De Simone case - a lie. On December 9, he is charged and taken into custody. The police will also question him several times about the murder of Teresa. However, since he has blood type 0, he is removed from the list of suspects.

Soon he comes into conflict with the law again and again and has to go to jail. He pleads guilty to several minor offences, but it turns out that he could not have committed them, among other things because he was in custody at the time.

On December 11, 1980, however, something happens that will trigger a nationwide media response and leave the investigators stunned. At that time, the feverish search for Teresa's murderer has been going on for more than a year - without results. The police are under enormous public pressure; the population cannot understand why no guilty party has yet been apprehended. On this cold December morning, Hodgson asks to see a priest. He confesses to him that he suffers from nightmares in which he sees the face of a woman he killed last year in Southampton. And he adds that it is particularly troubling for him because it was just the anniversary of the murder.

Sean Hodgson repeats this the next day to a prison guard and even completes a written confession. In the next two weeks, Hodgson will make further confessions and show the Southampton police investigators on the spot where he has deposited items belonging to Teresa De Simone. And he is said to know secret details that only the murderer could know. Unfortunately, no audio recordings of the interviews were made, and the paper documents could not be recovered until 2009.

On December 25 and 27, the prisoner confesses to two more murders, but it is proven that they never happened.

After a 15-day court hearing at Winchester Crown Court and a final nearly four-hour consultation, Sean Hodgson was finally found guilty of the murder of De Simone on February 5, 1982.

The course of events is reconstructed as follows: The accused, while intoxicated, broke into De Simone's car to steal it. There, he fell asleep on the back seat. When the young woman returned, she put her handbag in the back seat and woke Hodgson. He grabbed her, strangled her, and then raped her dead body. Then he fled with some of her belongings.

During the trial, the accused preferred not to make any statements and not to be cross-examined. His defence counsel is anxious to repeatedly point out to the court the special personality disorder that makes it doubtful whether his confession can really be used. After all, his client has confessed to about 200 crimes in which he cannot be involved. Among them even alleged murders that never happened. Nevertheless, the presiding judge Sheldon has no doubts whatsoever as to the accused's guilt, as he emphasises.

What is also not spoken during the trial is the fact that besides Hodgson and the unknown caller, five other people have confessed to the murder.

And on September 17, 1983 a certain David Lace will confess the murder to the police once again. In his testimony it is stated that he came to Southampton from Portsmouth on December 4 because he stole a backpack and cash from a nursing home where he lived. Lace was behind of the "Tom Tackle" when Savage dropped her friend off in the parking lot. When Teresa was sitting in the car, the young man knocked on the window and asked for the time and then forced his way into the car. Then he sat in the driver's seat next to De Simone and locked the doors. This was followed by the rape, after which Lace strangled the woman with the passenger seat belt. He hid for about 10 minutes before walking to the main station and taking the train back to Portsmouth.

Because Lace's statements about the victim's car and clothes are not correct and the discarded jewellery is not found at the location he gave, the police simply put the statement on file. Hodgson's defence is never informed of the confession.

It is only 26 years later, in 2008, that new evidence emerges that will put the case in a completely different light and lead to a renewed focus on the murder of Teresa De Simone.

Since his conviction in 1982, Sean Hodgson never tires of asserting his innocence. In 1998, an investigation is foiled because he falls seriously ill. His application for early release from prison after 16 years also fails, presumably because Hodgson keeps pointing out his innocence and thus proves to be "unreasonable". In 2008, he takes another chance and reacts to an advertisement in the magazine "Inside Time" by lawyers who specialise in appeal procedures. And he is indeed lucky! His case is taken over and finally there is movement in the matter.

After about four months, his legal counsel track down the samples from the crime scene, which were allegedly destroyed some 10 years earlier. Rag Chand, who voluntarily works as a lawyer for Sean, painstakingly assembles the details of the crime from newspaper clippings. During this detective work he comes across an apparently forgotten police archive in the Midlands in an industrial complex where the samples are found. On January 30, 2009, the reassuring news: the DNA analysis proves that the semen found does not come from Hodgson!

After a whole 27 years that Sean Hodgson innocently spent in prison, he is finally released as a fragile, pre-aged man! A sensation. As he steps outside the courthouse door, he suddenly stares into a thunderstorm of flashes, hears the deafening clicking of cameras and the babble of voices as the journalists waiting for him crowd around to get a comment from him. His brother is also waiting for him, hurries up and hugs Sean. For a long time, he does not let go of him, while tears of joy run down his face. A moving moment captured by the journalists from all over the country. The media interest confuses him - and so does the newly won freedom after more than a quarter of a century behind bars. The man, whose innocence has finally been proven, seems shaky, exhausted, and frail. Like a shadow next to his brother. Hodgson can see how much the years in prison have affected him. On the other hand, the release is a drama for Teresa's parents, because after 30 years they are deprived of the certainty that justice has been served for their daughter.

In March 2009, the Hampshire's Serious Crime Review Team will reopen the investigation into the murder of Teresa De Simone. A DNA comparison with the national database reveals something astonishing: apparently a sibling of the perpetrator is listed! This makes it possible to quickly narrow down a possible suspect. Since this one is unfortunately already dead, another of his siblings is tested as well. A procedure that was not possible at the time of the first trial. And: direct hit! The real culprit has been identified. It is David Lace.

For further clarification, the body of Lace, who had already accused himself of the murder of Teresa De Simone in 1983, will be exhumed at Kingston Cemetery in Portsmouth in August 2009. He had killed himself in December 1988 at the age of 26 in his hometown of Brixham, Devon. The reason: he was not able to live with his guilt any longer.

David Andrew Lace (or David Andrew Williams) was born in Portsmouth in 1962 and spent his youth in children's homes and residential groups. He is considered an aggressive loner and comes into conflict with the law for the first time at the age of 15. From this point on, the offences are relentless, mainly burglaries. He commits the murder of Teresa when he is just 17 years old. Repeatedly he turns to the police with confessions, but they do not believe him. In December 1988, he can no longer stand the gnawing guilt, gives away all his possessions and quits his job. On December 9 he is found dead - he has suffocated himself with a plastic bag over his head.

For Sean Hodgson, the 27 years in prison were extremely stressful. He has enormous problems living a life of freedom, and in December 2010 he comes into conflict with the law again. On October 27, 2012, the now 61-year-old will die of emphysema.

The Hampshire police will not reopen the flawed investigation that led to his conviction.

As a result of this case, a DNA comparison was carried out for all rape cases from before 1990. In 240 cases, the guilty parties were subsequently apprehended.

CHAPTER TWENTY:

Truants

"Pure evil. I will never change my mind about this." The Liverpool police investigator is still determined in his assessment twenty years after the case. "I looked into the face of evil that day," he continues. And even though the crime happened a good twenty years ago, he still expresses the horror he feels when he thinks back to the days in February 1993.

February 12, 1993 is the day that will become the most tragic in Denise Fergus's life, from the small town of Kirkby near Liverpool. Denise plans to go to the big shopping centre in Merseyside, north of Liverpool. A visit to the butcher is also planned. The mother is not sure if it is a good idea to take her two-year-old son James with her. Shopping with the happy, lively toddler, who is just about to discover the world, is usually quite stressful. Especially when he gets a temper tantrum and you're loaded with shopping bags.

For this reason, Denise asks her husband Ralph Bulger if he can look after their son this afternoon. But he has already promised to help his brother build new furniture that day. So, Denise takes her boy with her. James' vocabulary is still limited, but Ralph and he have a common goodbye word: "Ta-Ra!" He calls this out to his son as he leaves the house.

James is a kid who loves to make people laugh. Then he too is happy and this radiates over his whole, chubby face. He pinches his eyes together into small slits that peep boldly out from under the dark blond, dishevelled strands of hair. The little boy is music-loving and loves to dance to the hits of Michael Jackson.

So, Denise sets off with James to the Bootle Beach shopping centre in Merseyside. At first, the two of them stroll around a bit, the excited child pulls his mother by the hand here and there; but then Denise finally gets on with her shopping. She does not notice the excitement about a toddler leaving the shopping mall accompanied by two boys. His mother runs after him nervously through the mall and calls out for the child. Luckily, she can finally call him back at the door. However, the two boys have already disappeared again.

Nobody suspects at this point that they are already lying in wait again, because this afternoon they have thought up a very special game.

Meanwhile, Denise Fergus and her two-year-old son enter the butchers shop. She wants to buy chops here. Her son fidgets a little with her hand, so she lets go of him for a moment when she pays for the purchase at the cash desk. The mother is looking for suitable money and then has the meat served. It is only for this brief moment she doesn't have her son in sight - but it is enough to set in motion the devastating events of the following hours. James runs outside in front of the shop ...

Jon Venables and Robert Thompson are both just 10 years old in 1993, but they already have minds of their own. So, that day, they decided to skip school and go to the mall instead. They have a nice day - or at least that's what the two of them understand by it. First, they go on a pilfering tour and "organise" themselves some sweets among other things. They also steal blue model paint.

The boys have a bad start in life and grow up in a far from safe environment. The families live in one of the most run-down areas of England, which is also reflected in the family circumstances. Robert's father left the family five years ago, his mother has failed in life, drinks heavily, and suffers from depression. She has enormous problems to keep the family together and is completely overstrained with the care of her children. They "bit, beat and tortured each other", a welfare report later said. One boy is inconsolable when he is supposed to return to his family after a stay in a children's home and attempts suicide. A girl and even Robert have already attempted suicide themselves.

The family of Jon Venables is much less dysfunctional, but also here we are far away from normal conditions. The parents are also separated, the mother suffers from depression and thinks about suicide again and again. Jon's older brother and his younger sisters have severe learning disabilities, so they attend a special school. He himself is hyperactive and almost strangled another boy at school when he fought with him.

The fact that the first kidnapping of an infant that afternoon fails to work does not impress the two ten-year-olds. In any case, this game promises many more thrills than the usual rip-offs. That's why they're still on the lookout for a potential victim. Whether Jon and Robert already have a concrete plan at this point, what they want to do with the child, is unclear.

Around 3:35 pm, they discover the two-year-old James Bulger, who comes running excitedly out of the butcher's shop. Parents do not seem to be in sight, far or wide. This is exactly the moment Jon and Robert have been waiting for. They run off and talk to James. Then they take the boy by the hand who willingly walks with them towards the exit.

A short time later, Denise Fergus runs out of the shop and looks around: Where is her boy? When she cannot see him, she panics and runs off to look for him. She goes around to the left. A decision she will regret for the rest of her life. Because the three boys have turned right.

Later, she is shown the footage from a surveillance camera showing the three children. The time is 3:42 pm and everything seems harmonious. "I was relieved to see that James had gone with two other children. I thought they would eat sweets with him and treat him like a little brother," Fergus describes her feelings about the pictures later.

Robert and Jon have left the mall with the toddler and are walking towards the nearby canal. Here, the two young kidnappers want to put their plan into action: They want to throw little James in the water and let him drown. They lure him again and again to look at his own reflection in the water. But James refuses. He is still very small, but he knows water is dangerous. And he is afraid to lean so far over the edge.

The boy's refusal upsets Robert and Jon. They push him to the ground in rage, so violently that he hurts his head and also his face when he hits the hard, frozen floor. They are extremely frustrated that their plan is not working. That must have been the moment when the whole situation escalated, and Jon and Robert came up with something new. Something far more sinister. One of them kicks James in the ribs so that the child stands up, as one witness later states. Now they head for the railroad tracks.

On the approximately four-kilometre stretch to the tracks, the three boys meet a total of 38 people - but no one understands what is really going on here. Nobody stops the abduction, even though the two-year-old keeps calling for his mom and the injuries to his head are clearly visible. Also, his vocabulary is far too small to actually put into words what is happening to him. Because he sometimes laughs and gives the impression of being happy, it is probably thought to be arguments between brothers. Especially since Jon and Robert are stopped by passers-by, but they tell them that they have to take care of their little brother and that his injuries have been caused by a fall. That's why the three of them are repeatedly allowed to move on.

Finally, they reach the railway line near the town of Walton. Here, Jon and Robert are now putting their real plans into action. A plan so infinitely cruel that it will go down in British history as the most horrible criminal case, because the two ten-year-old boys torture little James to death.

First, they smear the blue model paint on the toddler's face, also staining themselves. Then, they take whatever is lying around and beat him with all their strength. In addition to bricks, this is also a ten-kilogram rusty iron bar. Again and again it descends upon his little head. As James lies on the ground, the two older boys continue to kick him. They catch him in the head and face. Several head injuries are so severe that each one could have been fatal. A total of ten different skull fractures have been reported. In between this, they also take James' shoes, trousers, and underpants off. They also inflict injuries in the genital area. In the end, the child's corpse shows 42 injuries, all of which were inflicted while he was still alive. The whole ordeal, in which the two probably let out all their aggression and frustration, lasts for over an hour, as the forensic medicine later states. The time frame is estimated from 5:30 p.m. to 6:45 p.m.

When life has finally left James' little body, Jon and Robert are probably overcome by some kind of intuition of a confused sense of injustice. Now they're trying to make the child's death look like an accident. They lay the body crosswise on the railway tracks and cover the head with stones. A few minutes later a freight train actually arrives. The train driver apparently does not notice the obstacle on the tracks and rolls over the small, defiled body. James is cut into pieces and the naked lower body is dragged along for several metres.

Afterwards Jon and Robert go home - as if nothing had ever happened.

It takes another two days before the body of the little boy is finally discovered. Valentine's Day is usually a happy day when you spend time with your loved ones. But in 1993, it is overshadowed by James' death. And it's also a difficult course for the police officers when they have to inform his parents about the event which has taken place.

The public's sympathy is already enormous at this point, but it will increase considerably and trigger a fierce discussion worldwide.

When James Bulger is buried on March 1, 15 days before his third birthday, 1,086 obituaries and condolences are published in the regional newspaper within a matter of days. Hundreds of thousands of bouquets of flowers are laid at the site where his body was found on the railway embankment - including Robert, one of his murderers.

Thanks to the recordings of the surveillance camera in the shopping centre, the kidnappers of James are quickly tracked down. It only takes a few days until Jon and Robert are finally caught. Since the blue model paint still sticks to their clothes, which is also on James' body, the noose around the underage perpetrators is tightened. In addition, the policemen discover blood on the boys' shoes; a DNA test finally reveals that it belongs to James. During the questioning of the two, in which they accuse each other of being the real culprit, photos are taken which are later published. For many people, it is a shock to look into the faces of two frightened children who are apparently responsible for the murder of little James.

As a result, there will be heated public debates about whether horror films may have been responsible for their deeds. At this time, there are already discussions about more and more explicit depictions of violence in movies and the fact that the father of one of the boys has the movie "Chucky 3" on his shelf is directly taken as an indication. In the film, which only received a licence for 18 years and above, a child or a child-sized doll is dismembered. However, it is often argued that something like this does not motivate one to do such a thing.

In the press, the gruesome murder is described as "the most horrible crime in the United Kingdom".

In the public debate, experts, moderators, laymen, and politicians argue. Some blame the social background and the parental neglect of the boys for the "dehumanisation" of the children, others consider such statements as class hatred. Some see the ten-year-old Thompson as the "mastermind" and the "true evil", whereas Venables is only a less intelligent follower. Still, others say that the focus on the question of "man or monster" does not go far enough. The mothers of the two perpetrators are harshly attacked by the public, not only verbally.

Finally, on November 7 1993, the main hearing begins at the Preston Crown Court in Liverpool. The extremely heated public mood will influence this trial from beginning to end. Although it had actually been agreed beforehand to maintain the anonymity of the two child defendants and to refer to them only as Child A and Child B, this soon tips over and the names become public. Furthermore, they are placed on specially made, elevated chairs, together with their social workers, as otherwise they would not have been able to look over the benches. This, in turn, gives the media representatives an excellent view of the two of them, which leads to comments on each of their movements and their entire behaviour.

Furthermore, the court decides to conduct the trial like a trial for adults - and not as if it were being decided on children. The judges and state officials thus appear in full, intimidating outfits. Parents are not allowed to sit with their boys. This scene alone shows that the entire force of state power is to be presented here - in a certain way it is a "show trial".

The trial lasts a total of 17 days, in which the mental state of Jon and Robert will be the subject of less than half an hour. The two cannot produce any evidence to exonerate them and so are both found guilty on November 24th, 1993. They are sentenced to a life sentence, which they are to spend in a juvenile detention centre. The minimum period is set at 8 years. This makes Venables and Thompson the youngest ever convicted murderers in English history.

Under the pressure of a petition signed by 300,000 people, even politics intervenes. The then Home Secretary, Michael Howard, personally demands an increase of the sentence to 15 years, but this is revised four years later by the House of Lords. In October 2000, the sentence of eight years is restored due to good behaviour.

A year later, on reaching their 18th birthday, Venables and Thompson are released and given a new identity. While Thompson has not been guilty of anything since then and is now supposed to live with a man, Venables has been in conflict with the law several times: for a fight in a drunken state, for drug possession, and twice for child pornography. The last time he was sent back to prison was in 2017. In court, it was discovered that he possessed 1,170 pornographic children's pictures, some which had extreme depictions, as well as instructions for "safe child sex", which also encourages serious maltreatment.

For the mother of little James, Denise Fergus, not a day has passed since February 12, 1993, without her wondering, "Could James still be alive if I hadn't let go of him?" She is still blaming herself because on the anniversary of her child's death she forgot to take the buggy with her, which she usually always had with her when she was out with him. If he had been in the buggy, he would not have been able to walk out of the butcher's shop ... On the 25th anniversary of the death of her son James, Denise Fergus has published a moving book entitled "Let him go". It is the attempt of a desperate mother, who still suffers from panic attacks and is severely traumatised, to save her son from being forgotten and to come to terms with the memories, which Fergus has not yet succeeded in doing. To this day, the police have not told her exactly what the two older boys did to her son. "I know only as much as my heart can handle."

UK TRUE CRIME

UK True Crime, hosted by Adam, is one of my favourite UK podcasts. Since 2016, there has been a new episode every Tuesday. The podcast also discusses lesser known British crime cases. Each episode is presented in a very likeable and down-to-earth way. The cases are varied in selection, very well researched, factually accurate and respectfully narrated in tone. If you don't know the podcast yet, then that should definitely change.

CRIME BOOKS UNLTD PODCAST

CRIME BOOKS UNLTD PODCAST by Catherine Yaffe Crime Books Unlimited is a podcast channel that interviews, promotes and discusses books that are in the crime genre. Featuring well known authors as well as independents, Crime Books Unltd is a channel for readers to find their next thriller, for writers to hear from experts in the crime field and for authors to reach a wider, new audience. Episodes are published bi-weekly and are available wherever you listen to your podcasts.

TRUE CRIME INTERNATIONAL:

**The successful book series
By Adrian Langenscheid**

Adrian's debut was released in June 2019. In the same month, the True Crime book by the as yet unknown author stormed to number 1 in the Amazon charts in the murder category. In fifteen True Crime short stories Adrian tells some of the most spectacular German criminal cases of the last decades.

After the surprise success and with the support of the podcast "True Crime", Langenscheid's second book "True Crime USA" was released almost half a year later in November 2019. The more comprehensive successor to the True Crime International book series continued the success of its predecessor.

Closing remarks by the author

Dear reader,

I hope that the short stories presented have moved you as much as they moved me while writing them. Let us all go through the world with attentive eyes for the needs of others, hopefully preventing many more tragedies.

Did you enjoy the book? If so, may I ask you one final favour? Authors, especially independent ones, need reviews, otherwise they won't be found on the incredibly large digital marketplace. As a writer, I've experienced how important ratings are in our digital age and how opinions can't be more conflicting. This is also the case now. Reviews decide on the success or failure of a book and audiobook. They decide whether a book is found and listened to. The step from no review to one already leads to a significantly increased visibility on marketplaces like Amazon. Not only do they boost sales, but they also make other readers aware of the book.

My dream is to dedicate a book to every country in the world and to collect the most spectacular True Crime cases for you. With only 5 minutes of your time and a positive review, you will help me to realise this dream.

Now right after the book is finished, you have the opportunity to do so.

I thank you in advance and wish you all the best

Yours Adrian Langenscheid